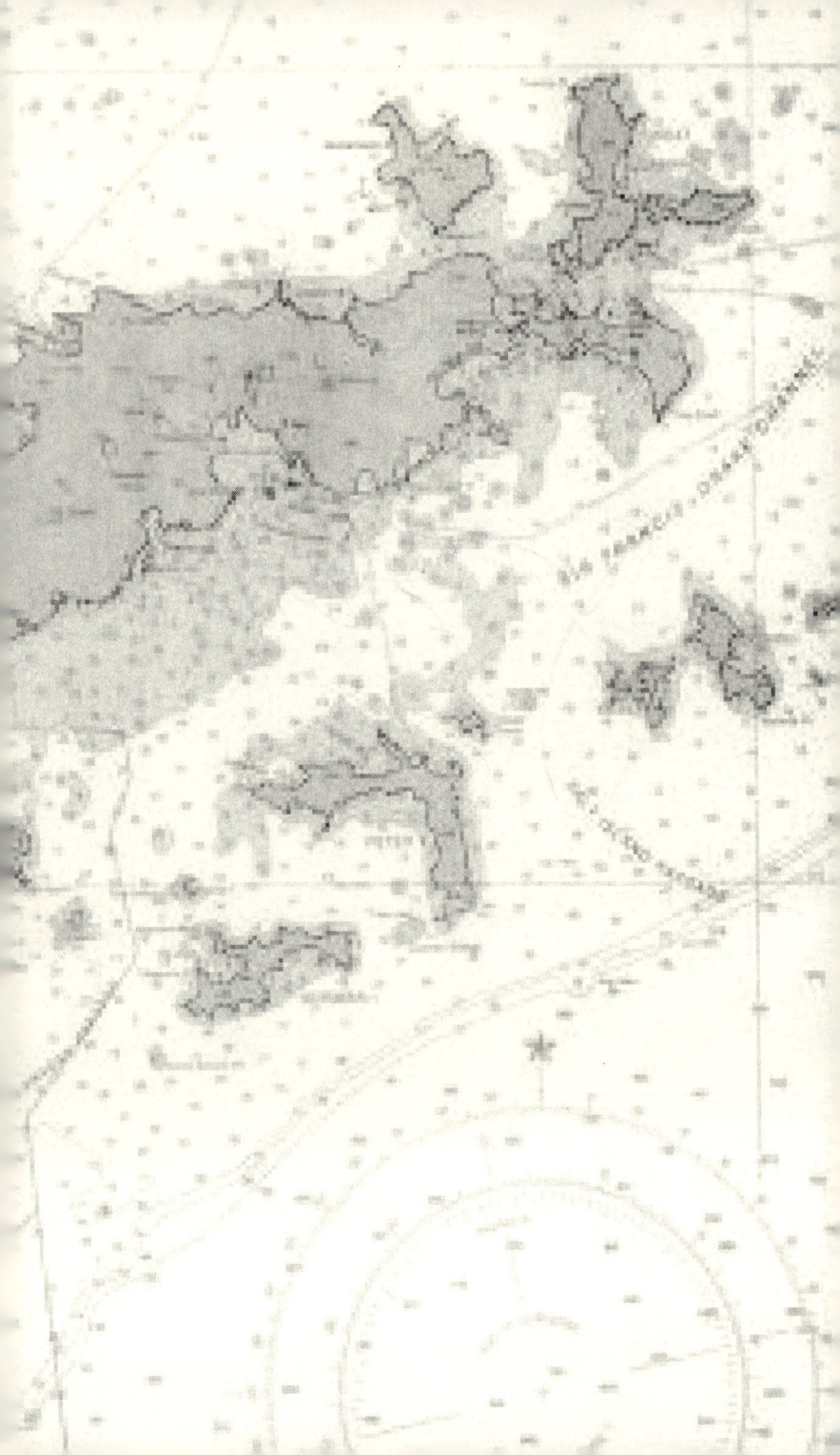

IF GOD STOPS WORKING

Rethinking Religion to Find
a Faith That's Real

———◆———

James Dale

The Chenault Publishing Group, LLC
www.chenaultpublishing.com

If God Stops Working: Rethinking Religion to Find a Faith That's Real
James Dale

www.ifgodstopsworking.com
www.jamesdaleauthor.com

Published by:

The Chenault Publishing Group, LLC
120 S. Denton Tap, Suite 450, Box 121
Coppell, Texas 75019
www.chenaultpublishing.com

10 9 8 7 6 5 4 3 2 1

First Edition © 2009 by James Dale
All rights reserved, including the right of reproduction in whole or in part
in any form without prior written permission from the publisher except in
the case of brief quotations embodied in critical articles and reviews.

Library of Congress Control Number: 2009910526

ISBN 978-0-9825626-0-4

Manufactured in the United States of America.
Also available in e-book and audio book formats.

Cover Design: Jed Rhien, Peterson Ray & Company
Illustrations: Tony Stubbs
Interior Design Concept: Brian Niemann, Niemann Design
Design & Production: Jay Zwerner, Zwerner Interactive

Your support for the author's rights is greatly appreciated.
Scanning, uploading, or distribution of this book or any of its
contents over the Internet or by other printed or electronic means without
express permission from the publisher is illegal and punishable by law.
Please purchase only authorized electronic versions.

*For Veda and Kerry who traveled before
For Vicki who travels with
And for Jessica and Mickey
who will forge their own paths after.*

Acknowledgements

Beyond all the many real-life characters who appear in the following chapters, I absolutely must begin by thanking my father and sister who, by encouraging me to share the words on these pages, graciously permitted me to tell a story that is as much theirs as it is mine. Beyond that, the list covers a broad gamut of friends, acquaintances, clergy persons, dozens of innocent and objective bystanders and others – all of whom contributed a word of direction here, a bit of guidance there. Of course, very special thanks goes to my wife Vicki who patiently tolerated my repeated stares off into oblivion as she carried on the conversations of daily life – she dealing with the practical and me connecting the dots between far-flung and disjointed ethereal thoughts while nodding my head in apparent agreement to whatever. Also, on the earthly plane, there is Bob and the other Bob and Alexander and Joe and Rufus and Gerry and Mark and Pat and Sue and Mike and Ron and Brian and Tony and the other Tony and Kathy and Jay and all the many folks at Starbucks who, night after night, waited until ten minutes after closing time to boot me out. And Scott and Scotty and Esther and Victory and Eric and Bert and Genla Kelsey Sangye and especially Ralph and Steph. And to Bryan and Scott and Jed and Carl. And to my marvelous old-soul children Jessica and Mickey for believing in me and being forever youthfully optimistic. A huge thanks goes to Mike and Danny and Devin for keeping me occupied – and therefore sane – through music as this all came together. And to the many, many others who – in blissful ignorance – said something quite off-hand or inadvertently mentioned a simple word here or there that sparked ideas or knitted far-flung and disparate notions together into coherent thoughts. And, perhaps most important, I owe a tremendous thank you to Mel Parker, of Mel Parker Books, who had the pragmatic experience and wisdom to patiently teach a guy who spent a quarter century learning to master the seven-word billboard the discipline required to let a story develop fully and on its own. Namaste.

Contents

Introduction	The Journey Begins	2
One	Brothers	14
Two	Not Me Did It	28
Three	Father Martin's Bell	38
Four	Dear God: You're Fired	49
Five	Jerry's Perfect Pets	62
Six	Of Deities and Dumpsters	74
Seven	Living Without *Without*	86
Eight	Letting Go of Loss	97
Nine	What Old People Know	108
Ten	Big Church, Little Church	119
Eleven	Cab Fare	132
Twelve	Wheels in Motion	145
Thirteen	For the Record	158
Fourteen	The Captain and Me	170
Fifteen	Who Speaks for God?	181
Sixteen	Children's Stories	196
Seventeen	Getting There from Here	209
Afterword	Signposts and Lessons	220

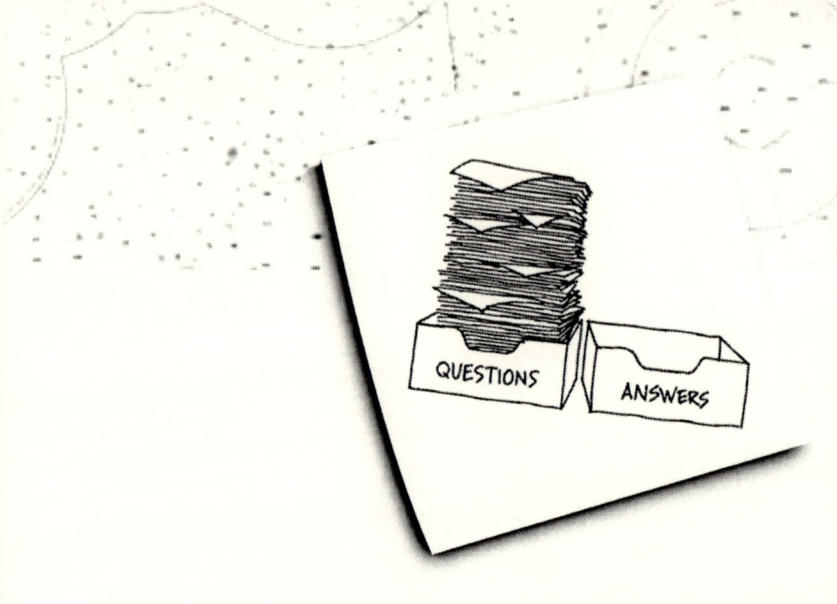

THE JOURNEY BEGINS

Late in the summer of 1988, I received a card in the mail from a lovely lady who lived in my hometown down on the Texas coast. It was a thoughtful note, sent with the very best of intentions, to share her condolences regarding the death of my younger brother who had died in a tragic flying accident several months earlier. I recall that the card had beautiful artwork and lots of flowers. It was innocent enough – a neat little way to let me know that she was thinking about my family and our loss. But on top of the pretty flowers and sweet sentiments, the card also put forth a sappy statement that was to have a deep and profound impact on my life from that day forward.

The card – no doubt crafted with little real thought by someone who had a creative quota to meet somewhere deep within the bowels of a gift card company – said something to the effect that *God needed a new statue for His garden.*

I kept nearly everything from that momentous event in my life – funeral and memorial programs, newspaper clippings, cards and letters, addresses from friends and well-wishers, stacks of pictures – all stowed neatly in a box for a later time when I could process everything in a greater, clearer context. One thing I'm sure I did not keep was that card. I distinctly remember the moment that I threw it in the trash – along with every bit of feeling I had toward whatever God I had known up to that point in my life. The statue idea made me nauseated. And angry.

My brother, two years younger and a promising Marine aviator, had flown a broken jet aircraft into the ground at nearly two hundred miles per hour some ninety seconds after takeoff on a muggy summer morning in North Carolina. He carried a full load of fuel and wing racks lined with practice bombs, so very little remained of either aircraft or pilot. What his death did leave behind was a loving young bride and a four-month-old daughter. His death also left the rest of us who knew him – who had grown up side-by-side with him – in complete terror, bewilderment and disbelief at how quickly bad things can happen in this fickle, transient life. In short, nothing had ever hit me that hard, before or since.

When I first heard the news of the accident, I remember thinking that, while this was sure to be a major milestone in my life, it was something I would get through relatively quickly – two or three weeks, tops, maybe a month – and move on to other things: my own wife, who was seven-months pregnant with our first child, my career, my home, my world. Now, just a few weeks after the casket had been lowered into the ground with a hollow-sounding *thunk,* and the bugle had blown out the last wispy notes of *Taps*, I was fast sinking into the darkest chasm I would ever know – with bleary eyes, shattered nerves, a total lack of focus and, not least, a freight car load of pain and shock that would overwhelm me out of the blue many times each day. I could not yet see that my world would never be anything like the same again. And the next two years would prove to be the toughest of the nearly fifty I have lived, steering me down the pathway toward alcohol and drug abuse, depression and worse.

Yet here was this innocent and dear woman presenting me with the sentiment that the God I had known my entire life had caused all of this to happen *for want of a new piece of statuary.*

What did I do? I dug deep. I prayed. I reached out as only the desperate can, trying to grasp for any answer, any salve, any balm that could soothe the raw, merciless pain and give me the peace I needed to feel whole again. I asked all the big and obvious questions. Why had this happened? Why did it have to be Kerry? Could death also happen to me, or to others whom I loved? When would the other shoe drop? Was God on a rampage? How was I supposed to process this massive event and file it all away in the greater context of my life? Everything I had learned about faith and religion – about God – in my twenty-eight years of living up to that time now failed me. When I reached into my big bag of God, there was nothing there.

Over a period of many months, I searched out and spoke with anyone whom I thought might be in a position to offer some clarity, a faint bit of insight, or the slightest sliver of resolution. I met with ministers, therapists and priests – all the older and wiser people whom I trusted from virtually every background and faith tradition. I got answers, at least to some degree, from all of them. But, in the end, when I boiled everything down hoping to find the handle that I could grasp in order to pull myself up from out of my pool of confusion and despair, I still came up with the same general notion: that God had somehow played a part in this – if not actively, then at least passively. It all seemed to have His tacit stamp of approval, if not His direct participation.

I had grown up in the Episcopal church, a good and rosy-cheeked boy who worked his way to the top of the acolyte roster by memorizing all the right things and checking off all the right boxes. I knew everything that my well-meaning parents and numerous parish priests could drill into to me. I earned a God and Country medal in Boy Scouts. Yet I still came up wanting at this crucial time in my life. I knew that God was omnipotent. I knew from years of Bible training and countless days in Sunday school that God kept a finger in all of my daily activities – that He knew, in fact, all the hairs on my head.

But now, as I wallowed through the most devastating period of my life, I could not find the peace and comfort – or answers – that I believed God would provide. Far from it – in fact, God actually seemed to be the perpetrator, the power behind it all.

God had simply stopped working.

Of course, in reality I know that God – whatever God is – never stops working. So before you relegate what I have to say to the trash heap alongside the lady's well-intentioned card, let me clarify that it was my understanding of God that failed me at that critical time in my life. And that's why I'm writing this book; to share what little I have learned with anyone who's reached for God at a time of crisis only to find that old ideas of God, and faith, and spirituality, can come up short when needed most.

As a well-trained acolyte, I knew the names of all the principal parts of the church. I knew the Latin names for all the polished silver accoutrements we used during Holy Communion. I could recite all sixty-six books of the Bible, in order, by heart. I knew the precise way in which to light the candles for Sunday worship services, and how much communion wine to pour into the chalice to be sure there was enough for the congregation – as well as one final healthy gulp for Father Martin. I could recite the Beatitudes from Matthew in the New Testament, and list all the Major and Minor Prophets from the Old Testament. Put flatly, I knew two creeds, Ten Commandments, and one Holy Trinity, inside and out.

But, strange as it may seem, I had somehow missed out on gaining a true and working understanding of the real nature of God. Specifically – and perhaps most tragically – I had missed the part where God loves me. Which, of course, God does. Or the part where God doesn't make bad things happen. Which, of course, God doesn't.

I quite simply had no real or meaningful understanding of the way that God works – or was supposed to work – in my life.

I am absolutely not qualified in any way to write a book about God, at least not in an ecclesiastical or liturgical or clerical sense. I am not a priest, or pastor, or rabbi, or monk, or imam or medicine man. I have never attended a seminary or earned any degrees in divinity. I don't wear robes or hats. In fact, I'm what many in today's contemporary religious world might call "unchurched" – whatever that means. I consider myself to be a deep spiritual seeker, which puts me smack in the heart of the largest (and fastest growing) spiritual subgroup in America – that ill-defined sect of folks who definitely believe in something but aren't necessarily affiliated with a particular church or faith.

What I am is just an ordinary guy who has lived through probably more than my fair share of life's hard hits – the fast balls and inside pitches that tend to whack some of us at the plate more often than others while friends and neighbors seem to trot easily and unscathed around the bases of everyday life. I'm a guy who lives out on the working end of faith – *just like you.* I deal with loss and pain and uncertainty and doubt and curiosity – *just like you.* I face day-to-day struggles out in the real world, searching for real peace and meaning and understanding – *just like you.*

By no means do I claim to have a corner on the market of suffering. I did not endure the Holocaust. I have not seen war. I live in the heart of what I still consider to be the greatest country on Earth, blessed with an abundance of everyday gifts and amenities. I have a loving family. I am healthy. But I have lived and loved and lost and learned through the many pains that mark the paths of our lives, and stopped to wonder at each place how, why and even *if* God plays a role. And if indeed He does, then what role is that, and how do we recognize it, and how does it help? How do God's answers or miracles or comforts reveal themselves? What is true and what is false about the many lessons I took away from my decades in organized religion? How do we separate the facts of God from the realities of Man so that we can have a true understanding of how God works when we drop to our knees to call out in a time of genuine pain and need?

The faith I practice today teaches me that some of us face life's tough challenges more often than others because we are blessed with the ability to share what we have learned with our fellow travelers. We are able to take the hard-won lessons and thin glimpses of wisdom that we have gained through our bumps and bruises and use them to lend an empathetic ear to family, coworkers and others who find themselves running up against the same obstacles we have faced and overcome. I also believe that all of life's tough challenges add up to create an exceptionally rich and meaningful life – and for that, I am grateful. I thank God – whatever God is – every day for the gifts and the lessons that I have been given. And I promise to use what little I know to help others I find in need around me to the best of my ability.

My faith also teaches me that we each learn an amazing amount from each other. We are all teachers, and we are all pupils. Practitioners of some Eastern faiths use the word *namaste* when greeting each other – one of many translations is "The God within me honors the God within you." I like that. It means that we can share our lives and lessons with each other and learn and grow together in God's world. It also means that we are free to re-think many of our old beliefs about God and how faith works day-in, day-out in our fast-paced and chaotic lives.

Over the past several years – with great welcome – a number of powerful voices have risen to be heard from the far left side of the religious spectrum. Prominent atheists are stepping out from behind the shadows and staking out a well-reasoned, intelligent and credible position for the non-existence of God. It's not hard to look at the conflicts raging out of control in many parts of the world today and call religion to account as the primary cause – and then draw the seemingly logical conclusion that if we could only do away with religion and its antiquated teachings, then all would be well and good. Perhaps only then would the world be whole and healthy.

On the other hand, there are many who – despite the nonstop advances that surround us in the fields of science and technology – point to all the chaos in the world as a reason to draw closer still to the fundamental teachings of ancient religions. Their argument could be that the craziness and insanity that seem to be escalating exponentially throughout the world serve to validate the infallibility and accuracy of religion's fatalistic predictions, and are quickly pushing us toward the inevitable doom of mankind. They seem to feel that we are truly in the end times.

What I see in each of these extremes is a coiled spring being pushed to its maximum limit of compression. Each camp is adhering rigidly to the old maxim that *when all you've got is a hammer, then every problem looks like a nail.* We either see religion as the cause of all of our problems or the answer to all of our prayers – literally. I believe this is because all of life's major issues – religion, politics, and morality – are largely defined by voices that shout out from the far extremes. Opinions in the middle are seldom heard, ill defined or simply too nebulous to be of interest. There is little news value in the muddling opinions of folks who live in the quiet center. There is nothing overly compelling about the mass of people who possess moderate views – and there are far too many of them anyway. No one cares.

But it is this middle ground – this fertile field that makes up the wide-open space between the absolute extremes of religion – where I believe the loudest voices in the discussion of God need to rise up today. That is one of the key ideas behind this book. I want to awaken the millions of shades of color that exist between black and white.

We live in a world of limitless color – millions of shades that run from the ultra-violet end of the visual spectrum to the infrared. Yet so many of us tend to frame up our discussions of God, spirituality and divinity in purely black or white terms. We see God in one way – or not at all. "Either you believe as I do, or you are a non-believer" is a common sentiment; there is one definitive, unchanging and unalterable way to look at God – *and that is all.* To a vast number of believers of all faiths, God is all or nothing, completely defined and unchangeable. I have had innumerable discussions with people from a great many religious persuasions who become completely thrown off track by the notion that there may be variations on the God they know. They have understood and accepted one concept of God their entire lives, and are unable to contemplate the infinite shades of God that can exist within their black-or-white, God-or-no-God perspective.

But to believe that God is either one way – as defined – or not at all is to subscribe to a very false dichotomy. I find it simply unreasonable for any one person – no different, in essence, than you or me – to have a complete or definitive understanding of God. And, in my view, anyone who says they do should be avoided like the proverbial plague. I have heard it said that any god who can die probably should. I take this to mean that if the supreme being of our universe isn't willing or able to stand up to some pretty serious scrutiny, then that god shows a less-than-perfect ability to bear the burden of perfection we place upon it. And if God is perfect, then surely He would know that our questioning and wandering would lead inevitably back to Him.

Being curious about God and about faith is always a good thing – *always.*

I hope to make it abundantly clear throughout this book that I believe in God – or at least some supernatural entity that fills that role in my life and the lives of others around me. I honestly believe that the world as we know it – and as we are yet to understand it – must have come from somewhere. There is simply far too much magic, marvel and mystery for our existence to have no root source. But I am also a firm holder of the middle ground. I do not blindly subscribe to conventional religion. My reason for this is because I think religion has largely lost its ability to ask questions – *it already thinks it knows all the answers.* And, to me, faith is all about questions – about learning, searching, and continuing to grow in our real and complete understanding of whatever our God is. Or what God *could* be.

And while I welcome the opposing view that atheism brings to the discussion – for without it there would be none – I think the preponderance of recent arguments fall short for two primary reasons. First, I believe it is disingenuous to think there could ever be a human civilization without some form of organized religion. Despite its faults, religion gives us a platform for common understanding – and could give us a great, unified springboard for continued learning and spiritual growth. Second, I think it is meaningless to dismantle an issue as fundamental as religion, simply saying that God doesn't exist, without offering up a viable alternative.

You can't take away a building's foundation and expect it not to collapse. Pure atheism fails to offer any explanation at all for our common existence – or the beauty, marvel and mystery of the physical world around us. It provides no concept whatsoever for why you are reading this book and pondering these issues at this very moment.

I feel closer in my religious views to these latter voices than I do to blinder-wearing religious extremists, to be sure. But that only means that I think they've missed the mark by a shorter distance.

There will be no end to religion – *however, religion should be open to change.*

God is not a delusion – *but our understanding of God might very well be.*

And God is great – *when shaped into something that truly makes sense.*

I certainly do not claim to have the answers to life's most profound mysteries. I certainly do not expect anyone to accept the same concept of God that I have – my understanding is unique to me. What I do have are questions. Lots and lots of them. For I believe that questions are what we need now, more so than answers. Answers abound. Questions are what move humankind forward in all our endeavors. Seeking, searching, exploring, questioning – and then starting all over again incorporating everything we have learned in our continuing journey; that is the cycle through which civilization moves forward.

The good news is, nothing bad can result from this questioning process. In fact, only one of two things will happen – and both are good. Either you will strengthen the faith you already have in whatever religion or God you know, or you will empower yourself to open up to new and different ideas that may take you to another place entirely – your very own personal understanding of a God that works in your life. The key to spiritual growth is to ask, seek and question. And then start that process all over again – adding richness and context and new perspective. There are no final answers.

I believe that we need religion, at least in some form, in our lives and in our world. And we need to realistically acknowledge the fact that religion will never simply vanish from human civilization. Like it or not, it's here to stay. As an institution, religion – any form of organized religion, anywhere in the world – forms a cornerstone of the very foundations of our Earthly existence. It's a fundamental part of the human experience – and it should be. Almost universally, religions do great things.

What I do think needs to change is our everyday working understanding of what religion is and what role it can realistically play in giving us the firm anchor we need to weather the storms of loss and strife and pain and anguish – and even celebration, joy and happiness – that make up the daily substance of our lives. We need to free ourselves to rethink the ways we view religion so that faith can be a meaningful tool for us when the you-know-what hits the fan and life takes an inevitable downward spiral. We need to strip away the ridiculous clutter and make religion into something real. We need to do this so that we can have a new and meaningful God that works, not just a belief in something that "sort of" works because we think it's supposed to. Most important, we need to understand the basic distinction between religion and God, for the two are unique and different. We need to cleave what we as humans have created God to be through religion from whatever the true nature of the Divine really is.

A key idea behind this book is that you, as a sovereign and perfectly whole individual, are blessed with a direct, one-to-one connection with your God. You hold hands, you mentally connect and you spiritually bond – *directly* – to your creator, whatever or whomever that is. You have as much of a direct connection to God as every other person alive on this planet today. Which means you are free to explore the idea of how God really works in your life on a parallel path with trained clergy and religion. In my thinking, a discussion such as this has to be largely driven by each of us as individuals and not necessarily by theologians. That's because a religious expert, by default, will always approach the challenge of truly understanding God from a religious perspective. It may be impossible – technically – for him or her to do otherwise.

I think the job of any good shepherd isn't to poke and prod his flock from field to field where they will be force-fed, but rather to guide and nurture them as they wander from field to field on their own in search of the nourishment they truly need. I have a great respect for the many people I have known who have devoted their lives to ministry – the vast majority are genuinely led by a calling to serve. But I have also known others who seem to have forgotten – or never learned – this simple key to raising a thriving, well-tended and healthy flock. In my view, even the most iconic of our spiritual leaders is no closer to God than you or me. We are all equal in God's eyes.

So, from that Everyman's perspective, I've written this book to give anyone who ventures down anything like the winding road I have traveled in my life the chance to share my experiences and hope. And to learn, like I have, that by giving up our old ideas of how and why God works, and claiming our right to rethink the true meanings and roles of religion, we can unlock the door to new routes of learning and equip ourselves to explore an incredible new and wondrous pathway through life.

It is my deepest hope that you will grow closer to the God you know as you journey along your own path.

One: Brothers

We learned to sail in a boat made of Styrofoam, my brother and I. Transplanted from the arid plains of West Texas to the muggy Mississippi coast in 1970, our family settled into a house under shady oaks a scant few hundred yards from the muddy waters of the Gulf of Mexico. Our new home sat quietly in a pleasant middle class neighborhood – a place of cypress trees, Spanish moss and palmettos – a planet away from the piñon trees and yucca plants we had known. But aside from the flora and the humidity, it was the presence of the ocean that made this new world a completely different and wonderful sort of place for us.

Except for one or two short trips to the coast to visit relatives early in our youth, we had never really known or seen the ocean. We found it exciting and alluring, beckoning to us the moment we first cast our eyes upon it and offering up the promise of pirates and pilgrims and treasures and tempests. For my brother and me, this new world by the seaside pumped blood into the veins of Fletcher Christian and Captain Ahab and Jason and his Argonauts, and brought to vivid life the fantastic stories of Jules Verne and Daniel Defoe. I realized instinctively then – as I have known since – that the ocean holds a special calling for me – *a siren's song if there ever was one* – and would forever play a deep and vital role in my spiritual life.

I read somewhere that nearly half of the people in America live and die within fifty miles of where they were born. I've also heard that something like half the world's population lives in close proximity to a coastline. Having lived both next to an ocean and far inland, I can say with great assurance that those who've never spent time near the shore may never know the majesty of what they have missed. For the sea is a perpetual living and breathing thing with its own shifting moods and temperament and personality. It becomes a partner of sorts – a continual companion that feeds its energy and life – its ever-changing currents and ebbs and flows – into everyone and everything it touches. Its rhythms and tides become our spiritual pulse, whether we know it or not. Unlike mountains, which erode and change at a pace far too slow to be noticed, an ocean remains in constant and visible flux – never the same from one moment to the next.

But Kerry and I, staring seaward from the marshy beaches of our new world at that wonderful time in our youth, did not see the profundity of all that. We merely saw adventure – and lots of it. Ours was not a shoreline of crashing waves and sand castles and beach umbrellas, but rather a narrow tidal strand of mud and broken bits of shell and sand and grassy reeds. Its murky waters were gentle and easy for the most part. Peering far off to the south, one could see why; the barrier islands that hem in the Mississippi Sound ran like an unbroken length of thin white thread from east to west as far as the eye could see. To the left, Petit Bois Island appeared on the far-distant horizon. In the middle lay Horn Island, and then the Ship Islands and Cat Island far off to the south and right of that. Bearing west from there, a string of smaller islands and sand-bars ran all the way to the ever-shifting Mississippi Delta that juts outward like a chin from the southeast corner of Louisiana. This chain of islands serves to block the coast from the Gulf's deep-rolling swells and creates a sheltered twenty-mile-wide playground for fishermen, shrimpers and oystermen – and soon-to-be explorers like us.

No sooner had the moving van been unloaded than our mother issued a decree that we would learn to sail. No youth could grow up in such a place, she said, and not do so. All the older boys in our neighborhood – even those too young to drive a car – had boats of one kind or another. Many had flat-bottomed skiffs with small outboards that they used to run crab traps out in the sound for extra money – local marinas paid a dime for each live crab. Others had sailboats – zippy little Hobie cats and only slightly less dashing Sunfishes and Seahorses. Ever the supportive sportsman, our father had spotted an ad in a magazine that offered a complete sailboat for one hundred dollars and the proof-of-purchase tabs from ten cartons of cigarettes. Taking one for the home team, he puffed away for months on end, and one day, as eagerly expected, a large cardboard box arrived at our front door.

The carton contained bundles of cords and lines and bags of hardware. And lengths of aluminum tubing and wooden slats and boards of various sizes and shapes. And a green and white-striped nylon sail emblazoned with the cigarette brand – KOOL®. And, of course, there was the craft itself, which was little more than a two-inch-thick Styrofoam shell perhaps ten feet long and a foot deep. Standing as a family around the odd parts spread about the garage floor, our mother took one look and summarily christened the new boat the *Ice Chest*.

Along with the Ice Chest came two simple documents: one, the directions for assembly, and the other – a small, single-folded brochure – a complete set of sailing instructions. Looking back, I find it amazing to think that all of humanity's accumulated knowledge of how to move vessels of all shapes and sizes through the oceans of the world using wind-power alone – a science first pioneered by the ancient Phoenicians as they plied their circular trading routes through the eastern Mediterranean, then refined over the centuries by a hundred Magellans in their caravels of global exploration, then tuned to near perfection by the masters of the sleek clippers that raced around Cape Horn during the days of the Gold Rush, and finally mastered by the yachtsmen of powerful sloops over the past century – could be boiled down to a few simple drawings and several numbered steps. But there it was. And no sooner had we deciphered the strange names of the many parts and assembled the mast, boom, sheet, halyard, tiller, rudder and dagger board than we – armed with our simple guidelines – set out to master the feat of maneuvering the Ice Chest through the water under sail. We launched it in the muddy bayou that ran from the back of our home straight out to the bay several hundred yards away and off we went.

Today, I know that sailing – no matter how complicated it might seem to the novice – is really quite simple. There are three basic points of sail – running, tacking and reaching – and these are all one needs to know to get from one place to another on any boat anywhere in the world. We either set our sails wide out to let the wind push with brute force from behind – a *run* – or trim them in tightly to the boat's centerline to rise like a wing in flight up close to the direction of the wind – a *tack*. And *reaching* is but a set of variations-on-a-theme of everything in-between. What separates an America's Cup skipper from a thousand duffing amateurs are the skills and instincts – developed through study, practice, and trial and error over decades – that go into mastering the host of subtle nuances that affect these three basic points of sail.

Over the coming years, Kerry and I were to learn – and somewhat perfect – those three general points of sail to propel the Ice Chest through a thousand miles of nautical adventure. The broad estuary of the Pascagoula River and the many wide-open square miles to the west and south became our playground. In time, we learned to recognize by sight the many landmarks and reference points that served to fix our position in the grander scope of our sailing universe – a staggered line of tilting poles placed at hundred-yard intervals marked a channel, a stand of trees on a sandy bluff gave us a rough bearing to steer for home, a patch of colorfully painted milk jugs indicated a mine-field of crab traps set in deeper waters, and a faint dip in the thin line of marsh grass signaled the entrance to the winding canal that led back to the barnacle-encrusted boat slip at the rear of our home.

We learned to sense the breeze and waves to avoid letting ourselves slip too far downwind – an act that required hours of tacking back into the wind, often against the current, to regain our starting point. We learned to trim the simple lateen-rigged sail just to the point of spilling its air to snatch up the full power of the wind and send the shallow craft screaming across the tops of the waves on a broad reach. We learned how to pull up the battered dagger board to allow ourselves to drift clear of the muddy shoals and oyster beds we inevitably discovered close-in along the shoreline. And we learned to scull the craft along using the rudder alone when the winds died, as they frequently did.

We tried many times without success to pilot our tiny craft all the way out to the barrier islands; even in the freshest of breezes the trip would have meant hours of plowing the fragile vessel through higher waves in deeper water.

We did visit many times a smaller island five or so miles out that hosted the ruins of a lighthouse built around the time of the Civil War. We flipped the boat a hundred times – sometimes by accident, quite often on purpose – and worked as a team to perfect the simple drill of righting it again and climbing back aboard. Each time, we gathered up our floating gear – an oar, a bucket, the various lines – bailed out the water and trimmed in the sail to start ourselves underway again.

Eventually, we mastered the performance characteristics of the Ice Chest in every way, learning that by carefully balancing our weight so that the lee side of the boat stayed just above the waterline and hauling in tightly on the sail, we could harness a fresh puff of breeze and sprint for great distances, letting loose the sheet to dump the wind only when a high-speed spill became inevitable. I recall one occasion when – steering the boat and leaning far out on the high side – I looked down to see Kerry leaning out in perfect symmetry on the low side, the hair on the back of his head skipping across the water as it zipped past. Suddenly, with no warning at all, a large black fin sprang from the water just a few feet in front of him – a porpoise. In one swift motion, and with eyes like saucers, he lifted himself up and flung himself into the boat. My reaction was a few seconds slower and we flipped over to windward almost instantly. After quickly righting the boat and climbing back aboard, we luffed the sail, letting it flap noisily in the breeze, and allowed ourselves to drift slowly downwind as we watched one, then two, and then an entire pod of porpoises come to play all around us.

On another voyage, as I zigzagged the boat through a line of crab trap buoys – much like a racecar driver veering back and forth through cones on a test track – Kerry came up with the bold idea to reach out and grab one, thinking we might easily drag it along with us. With precision timing, he snatched a line just beneath a painted milk jug – then disappeared just as quickly in a blur over the side. We learned that day that crabbers anchored their traps with cinder blocks.

All in all, we fulfilled our mother's edict to the fullest during our years with the Ice Chest. We knew little of the official jargon or arts of the mariner – the precise names for parts of our boat or knots or maneuvers or, for that matter, any of the official rules of the road that govern boats at sea. Late one hazy afternoon, we allowed a fresh westerly to push us far to the east of our usual sailing grounds and into the middle of a deep channel used by large warships traveling to and from the big naval shipyard at Pascagoula. We sat mesmerized as a sleek destroyer zoomed up out of nowhere, blasted its horn and passed us less than a hundred yards away, nearly swamping us with her wake. I remember looking up to see an officer at the railing of the bridge nodding back at us and smiling. Perhaps he, too, had first taken to the sea in a small boat made from Styrofoam.

But these were changing times for both of us. And as we set out to chart our own individual courses through adolescence, we began to follow our own points of sail. We were quite different in many ways, Kerry and I. Not only in our passions and interests but physically, as well. He was stout and handsome, with curly blonde hair and brilliant blue eyes and a perfect, solid face. Stockier and far more muscular than I, he was a natural and gifted athlete. So while I began to dabble in music and writing and other creative pursuits, he steered toward sports. As the months and years passed, we gathered up our own networks of friends and, as teens do, embarked off on our own social agendas. Yet we remained as brothers always – joined in our lives, united in our shared adventures, bonded by our times aboard the Ice Chest.

By some quirky twist of fate – or strange rules of zoning – we always attended different schools. Not only in Mississippi, but also later in the mid Seventies when our family moved to Houston. As a result, we spun off into our own worlds, with very little overlap in friends and activities. We grew more different still – and yet remained very much the same. Raising two children of my own, I have come to believe that perhaps ninety percent of what we are to become in life is already with us at birth. The very best that a parent can do is recognize each child's unique traits, gifts and challenges, and work to shape them into something generally positive that will turn our offspring into happy, well-adjusted and productive adults.

So, while I marched down the road toward band and the school newspaper, Kerry took to the track. While I lived obscurely in the middle of my pack of classmates, he grew to become a leader – ultimately president of his high school senior class. While I migrated toward liberal arts studies at a state college, he gravitated toward business at prestigious Baylor University. And, while I donned my share of Pink Floyd and Led Zeppelin t-shirts, he took to cowboy hats and boots.

Looking back, I believe it was exactly these differences – some subtle and others quite dramatic – that led us to complement each other so neatly in our lives. We remained close despite everything, and made trips throughout our college years to visit each other on weekends, often startling our friends by our contrasts. I respected and admired him and took great pride in him and told him so on many occasions. And he shared with me that he envied my uniqueness and creativity and admired me, too. Such is the bond between brothers; even though we set our own courses through life, we inspired each other to become better people. We pushed and encouraged each other. I know that Kerry made me better than I would have been on my own. I'd like to think I did the same for him.

Interestingly, I was the one who first had the idea of joining the military and learning to fly. In my senior year of college, with no firm plans after graduation – or even an official degree plan – I happened past a Navy recruiting table on campus. Impressed with the sharp white uniforms and the prospect of flying sleek, silver jet fighters, I applied and was accepted to Aviation Officers Candidate School (AOCS). With all the discipline I could muster, I created structure around my life, exercising daily and studying with a passion. Over a period of months, I passed all the physicals and aced the very demanding tests. But it was not to be; a month before graduation, I received a letter from the Navy informing me that, without a technical degree, naval aviation would not be an option for me. This was 1983, and a healthy recession had set in, greatly expanding the Navy's pool of potential "sky drivers." As a consolation prize, they offered me a commission as a public affairs officer, which I politely declined. Writing press releases could never be the same as flying.

Whether my non-starter with the military had any influence over my brother's plans is unknown to me, but by the next year he was enrolled in the Platoon Leaders Course (PLC) of the United States Marine Corps – a program for college students to spend two summers working toward a commission after graduation. These became intensely serious years for him, and we shared them together through almost-daily letters and phone calls – me offering what support and encouragement I could. The day he graduated, he also received his commission as a newly minted second lieutenant. It was an honor for me – along with our mother – to pin shiny gold "butter bars" on the shoulders of his crisp new officer's dress blues.

We followed each other closely during the nascent years of our careers – me as a fledgling advertising writer and he, having racked up high scores at the Marine Corps Basic School, opting for aviation. Perhaps it was a yearning to range freely in a milieu without boundaries – as we had done as boys in our boat made from Styrofoam – that drew him to flying. Or maybe it was a desire to push himself to his absolute physical and mental limits. But over a strenuous period of many months, he moved from one training base to another – including Pensacola, Florida, where he undoubtedly flew over the very waters we plied as boys in the Ice Chest. I very clearly recall the day he called me in my small office to tell me he had completed his carrier qualifications aboard the ancient USS Lexington cruising through the Gulf of Mexico to earn the coveted "wings of gold" that established him as a fully qualified naval aviator. I closed the door and sat cross-legged on my desk as we laughed and celebrated together – he with a freshly uncorked bottle of champagne on his end.

Through all of the months and moves that followed, and despite the distances, we remained close. He served as the best man at my wedding; two years later, I returned the honor. On each occasion, we chartered a thirty-six-foot sloop to take our respective bachelor parties out for a midnight cruise across the moonlit bay that sprawled southward from our family's weekend home on the coast. As the revelers alternately drank and hugged the railing, Kerry and I remained at the helm – a large chrome wheel in place of the tiny wooden tiller we had mastered aboard the Ice Chest – once again testing our skills with the three basic points of sail and soaking in the thrill of piloting a fast-moving boat through fresh, warm breezes on wide-open water.

I remember his late-night call from the Marine Corps air station at Cherry Point, North Carolina, in mid-1987 to share with me the news that he and his new bride were expecting their first child. Six months later, I made it a special point to wait until the middle of the night to call and share my own similar news. Months later, I received another late-night call – this time to announce the birth of his daughter. I made a note to call him – again late at night – when the time came to share my own new arrival.

It was a call I would never make.

Driven to excel in everything he did, Kerry had finished at the top of his flight-training class and was therefore able to choose the type of aircraft he wished to fly. Filled with Marine Corps "guts and glory," or perhaps urged on to the ultimate challenge by higher-ups and peers, he opted for the Marines' most coveted aviation asset – the AV/8B Harrier. It was – and unfortunately remains – a unique aircraft in the military arsenal, with its ability to take off and land vertically simply by floating on jets of hot engine gasses – a feat "Scarrier" pilots equate to balancing an elephant on the head of a pin. But it is also the most accident-prone plane in the inventory by far – a "widow maker" – having killed perhaps fifty pilots in individual accidents over the past thirty-plus years. At 7:15 a.m. on July 13, 1988, my brother, 1st Lt. Kerry Duane Dale, became Harrier casualty number twenty-five.

Through all of my experiences with Kerry – his life and his death – I have learned that we each exist as the sum total of all the events that make up our lives. There can be nothing more – or nothing less – for any of us. We are who we are because of the people we have known, the places we have been, and the triumphs and tragedies we have endured. Kerry was one component of my life – one of ten thousand distinct pieces that have joined together over time to create the whole person that I am today. He is a part of me – a big one – that came, played a major role in shaping me, and then disappeared virtually overnight into the vapor of my history.

When I sat down many years ago to take my first formal course in navigation – learning to view channel markers, milk jugs and trees on a bluff in terms of latitude, longitude, compass points, bearings, tracks and nautical miles – the instructor began by telling us *in order to know where you're going you first have to know where you've been.* This I believe to be true – not only for moving a boat through the water or an airplane through the sky, but in our spiritual lives, as well. Regardless of how many people claim to talk with God directly on regular basis, I have yet to see His hand actively at work in my life in the present tense – and I've learned better than to ask some supernatural entity to grant me wishes or tell me what will happen tomorrow. But I know with complete certainty that I can look back over the decades of my life and see the force of some immense power beyond myself filling an important and meaningful role in my world.

To me, the works of God – presented via the steady stream of spiritual lessons I receive almost daily – can be viewed only in hindsight. It is only by looking backward through the many seasons of my life that I have recognized the epiphanies that give shape and form and meaning to God and demonstrate His actions and presence. It is these lessons and experiences – the events that occur in each of our lives that make us who we are – that can best help us to understand how the idea of God should work most positively in the world we occupy at present – and in the days that lie ahead of us, as well. Meaning exists – in abundance – if we are only brave enough to look. Like a breeze on our cheeks, our life experiences help us to determine the proper points of sail.

It is a certainty that none of us can predict what will happen tomorrow, or even later today; if we could, wouldn't we? There may be another 9/11. A loved one or friend may leave us suddenly. A new treasure may enter or an old one depart. The global economy may flip over and flounder as easily as two boys in a shallow boat made from Styrofoam, leaving life as we know it in shambles. We simply have no way of knowing – and God will not say. As unexpected events happen, each of us must turn inward to search within the confines of our own minds to find relevance, meaning and insights. All of life – surely all of spirituality – is built upon our ability to look behind us. So that we can know where we are going as we move forward toward greater understanding.

Several years ago, I attended a high school graduation ceremony for my niece – my brother's daughter – whom I had not seen in person for perhaps eight years. I was stunned by her beauty, poise, elegance and charm – but also by her expressions and mannerisms. Looking into her eyes, I immediately saw the beaming smile of a boy with curly blonde locks and tanned shoulders aboard a boat made from Styrofoam in the carefree waters of the Mississippi Sound. I gave her a few pictures I had recently discovered of Kerry in his youth – images she had never seen of a father she never knew. She glanced at them briefly and smiled and thanked me and then stuffed them away in her purse. I know that some day she will look at them again and perhaps want to know more. But for the moment, her gift to me was far greater than mine to her.

Afterward, I thought of the many times we ventured too far from shore or too far downwind – her father and I – returning home late for dinner and covered with the salt crust of the sea only to hear our mother ask *where have you been?* Our answer was always the same – searching, seeking, and going where the wind would take us. We were doing what boys do in a tiny boat made from Styrofoam on the broad sweeps of the Mississippi Sound – learning about nature and beauty and the wind and the seas – the rich fullness of life in the Creator's bold and adventurous world. We were sharing it for the moment, knowing not – or caring not – what the future held.

Sailing still makes up a large part of my life. Along with the many other things I have today – family, friends and experiences – it completes me and makes me who I am. I have graduated to boats of bigger sizes over the years and have chartered large and seemingly complicated vessels to sail in many parts of the world. But no matter what boat I sail, or where, I am able to think back to the simple set of guidelines we received with the Ice Chest and remember that sailing – all of life, really – is very simple. I have already been given many of the lessons I need to help me understand the way that God works for me. I have been given experiences – the events, people and places – that define me – and God. And more are sure to come, as long as I am willing to look behind me – across my stern – to see them.

Today, when I sail by myself, often in the evenings, I think back to the many wonderful adventures my brother and I shared during our time together in a small, well-worn and dented boat made from Styrofoam, stained by the gulf's muddy waters and – by the time we had outgrown her – patched from stem to stern with gray duct tape. I am forever grateful that he was a part of my world and I was a part of his.

He sails with me still.

Two: Not Me Did It

I've been blessed enough by the Creator to share my home with two children. I know these two – have seen them go through every change imaginable from the moment I helped to draw them each from their mother's womb. I could spot them instantly in the largest crowd or find either of them by scent in a darkened room. They are my daughter and son and are among the greatest gifts I have received in my life. But there is another little one who resides in my home whom I've never met. I speculate that he (for the sake of discussion, let's assume that this being is a he) is relatively young because he showed up just a couple of years after my oldest child was born. And it's pure guesswork that he's at least something like a child because I've never actually laid eyes on his physical being. The one thing that I do know with a fair bit of certainty about this entity is what he does or doesn't do, which seems to be either an awful lot or nothing at all. And I know his name: Not Me.

I learned everything I know about Not Me from my two actual real-life children – and through the continual references either or both of them have made to Not Me over the past fifteen or so years.

Who left the car door ajar so that the battery is now run down and the engine won't start? Not Me did it.

Who keeps leaving empty milk jugs – and some not quite empty with maybe a half a glass left – in the refrigerator alongside a freshly opened jug? Not Me does.

Who forgets to put up the screen on the laundry room door so that the dogs can get in and root around for snacks in the cats' litter box? You can bet that Not Me is the culprit every time.

And, as often as Not Me is guilty of doing something, he's also guilty of not doing anything at all. *Who forgot to empty the litter box so that there wouldn't be any little snacks for the dogs to enjoy?* You guessed it: Not Me.

Around my house, Not Me has become a general-purpose combination of scapegoat, punching bag and Tooth Fairy who can be pointed to – quite confidently and with great frequency – for just about any situation that arises. He's completely invisible, so nobody's ever actually seen him do or not do anything. Therefore, it can't be proved that he's not the guilty party. And, since he never says a word, it's pretty hard for him to explain away his involvement, or lack thereof, in all of these activities. Yet Not Me takes the heat for pretty much everything that can possibly go wrong around our home. He rarely gets credit for the good things that might happen, though I suppose there's nothing that would prevent him from receiving accolades if they are deserved. Either way, he's the instant answer whenever it's convenient – the go-to guy when things can't be explained any other way.

Much like God.

We give God far too much credit, and way too much blame, for the endless list of things that happen to us and to others around us as we meander through the passing days of our lives. Not knowing what else to say when a friend's loved one dies, we offer up the odd sentiment that *this must be God's Will* and it's not for us to understand or question the reasoning behind that. Perplexed when people who are dear to us are faced with seemingly random acts of misfortune – bankruptcy, divorce, illness or worse – we default back to the easy answer: that *everything is somehow part of God's Master Plan* for our lives. Confused over the sudden loss of a job or family pet or relationship, we point to the heavens and grudgingly accept that *God must have caused all of this* for some reason that we're not privileged enough to know or that is many levels removed from our mortal ability to comprehend.

Several years ago in a city not far from where I live, a deranged man walked into a church late one afternoon just as a group of teenagers was wrapping up whatever teens do at church in the afternoon, pulled out a gun and opened fire, killing several and wounding many others before he was cornered and subdued by police officers. The smoke hadn't cleared the building before news crews arrived on the scene, cameras at the ready. They plugged in their microphones, hoisted their antennas and went on-air live, just in time for the evening broadcasts.

As the cops and coroners went about stringing yellow tape and processing the crime scene, the news crews waded into the milling crowd – sticking cameras and microphones into the faces of anyone who could offer an insight into the gore and carnage that had occurred just moments earlier. I very clearly recall the face of one woman who had raced to the church the moment she got word of the gunfire to make sure her own teen was safe in this sacred space which, by definition, promised safety, security and sanctuary.

Her teen was, in fact, among the lucky ones who were spared. And she was understandably gleeful and thankful for this as she answered the queries tossed her way by an over-caffeinated news reporter. God must surely have heard her prayers and reached down to protect her precious child, keeping him out of harm's way as the bullets flew this way and that. She practically fell to her knees in thankful praise that God had spared her son. And that was all pretty much well and good.

In the background, however, over her shoulder but still within the camera's field of view, another mother was receiving the news that her child was among those killed. I will never forget the look of shocked horror and confusion that came across her face, even as others around her alternately jumped for joy or fell prostrate in praise. Caught up in the excitement of the moment, a reporter moved in quickly for a once-in-a lifetime interview. Luckily, before the reporter could lift her microphone, the subject was whisked away by friends, stunned expression and all. Thank God.

You could read – through the pain in her eyes – the thoughts that were skittering through her mind at that exact moment. *Why did God save that other woman's child and not mine? If God loves her and her family that much, am I now to believe that God does not love me or my family? Have I not made the cut in God's eyes? What have I done wrong? Is God punishing me?*

Despite the shock and horror of a story like this, its theme is fairly common: we feel that God is somehow pushing the buttons at every tragedy – or gripping the levers of every blessing. God makes bad things happen, and God makes good things happen, and God actively decides – like an old man at a chess table on a sunny sidewalk at the edge of Heaven's big park – who lives and who dies and which family suffers and which businesses succeed or fail.

I switched on the radio in the car one morning not long ago just in time to hear a program featuring children from a local elementary school – a religious one – talking about working and studying for an upcoming test. To a child, they described how they would pray to God the night before to help them get good grades. Not much was said about studying, but a pretty heavy emphasis was placed on praying. I didn't catch Part II of the program in the following days to find out how they all did, but I feel certain that some kid in the group feels failed by the Almighty.

I am amazed at how many situations we face in our everyday lives where God is seemingly responsible for directing the myriad details of our very existence. You may ask, *you mean He isn't?* And there's the rub; we're all conditioned from our youngest years to believe that God handles all the details. That he's the Man with the Plan. That He sits at the giant decision table of our lives and controls everything that happens, or doesn't happen... every good thing, every bad thing, every success, every failure... every miracle, every disaster. He is our final judge, right? According to Pat Robertson and Jerry Falwell, God caused the tragedy of 9/11 to punish gays and feminists. And the Big Guy upstairs was gracious enough to spare the life of Oral Roberts because he raised something like eight million dollars in time to meet a heavenly deadline.

Far from being a benevolent creator, a God that behaves in this way – making arbitrary decisions based on some reasoning that we cannot understand or that makes no sense to us but that can affect our lives in such profound ways – is behaving much more like a rotten child who needs a time-out than some supreme being who manages our world with structure, love, form and reason. This excuse that God is behind everything – that He masterminds every tragedy or blessing, or at the very least allows all these things to happen for some divine purpose that we are not entitled to know or wise enough to understand – gives us an easy out. It enables us to rationalize things that simply aren't rational and explain away events that fall outside the bounds of explanation. *God gives us a ready-made Not Me.*

So God and Not Me have much in common. But there is one area where they are quite different: while we can't really put a finger on what Not Me looks like, or thinks like or acts like, we think we've got a pretty good handle on God. We trust that we know how God works. We believe that He will listen directly to our requests and perhaps grant them. God will listen to us as we explain what we want – and how we want it and when. In a way, God is like Santa Claus; if we've been good, then we can count on lots of treats in our stockings, but if we haven't, then we're in for a few lumps of coal. In an ethereal sense, I do very much believe that there is some omnipresent power at work in our universe that steers the course of Earthly events. I also believe that, in some strange way, we actually do receive usually those things that we need – but not always those things we want – in life. And the laws of karma are as right as the Golden Rule when we discover that good vibes sent out typically result in good vibes bouncing back.

I think that maybe we should avoid trying to define God. Because when we do, we are – virtually by definition – limiting God. When we describe how we think God can or should respond to some Earthly query, then we're presenting God with multiple-choice options. We want something one way or the other. And, by doing this, we unknowingly write ourselves out of a gift that may be unknown or unrecognized to us – we fail to leave ourselves open to the options of *all or none of the above.* Maybe we sort of just need to let God be God and leave it at that. And then get on about living in this world and doing the best we can without having to fall back on some Not Me explanation every time life takes some strange or unexpected turn. We need to stop defining God, *because only then can we stop blaming God.*

It has taken many years and a lot of painful bumps and bruises for me to learn that God doesn't work like a puppet master in some grand cosmic theater. Who would want to believe in a God that does? I choose to believe that God has nothing whatsoever to do with creating the tragedies around us. God doesn't cause tsunamis or earthquakes or bring down tornadoes and hurricanes to devastate the Earth. God doesn't make wars or create diseases. These are all natural things at best, man-made things at worst, and happen easily enough all by themselves without any intervention from the divine world.

So if God doesn't pull the strings in some Earth-bound puppet show, then what are we to make of the fact that one person dies in a bizarre church shooting and another person, standing perhaps just a few feet away, doesn't? First, we should let God off the hook for being all-knowing and omnipotent. If there really is some action-oriented, hands-on God, then I think He could be either all-loving or all-powerful – but not both. Wouldn't an all-loving God use infinite power to keep bad things from happening to His beloved creatures? And wouldn't an all-powerful God make an unlimited effort to do only good and not bad in our lives if He loves us completely? Let's also simply accept the fact that *life just happens* – it's full of randomness. We can analyze any occurrence in the world around us and put God's signature on it if we really want to. We give God credit for good things, bad things and everything in between. We want to attribute everything to something. Why? Because it's tough for us, as humans, to understand that sometimes it simply is what it is – and nothing more.

I have a great respect for all of the early philosophers and teachers who wrote much of what we commonly refer to as divine scripture. No doubt there is a lot of really great knowledge contained in those fragile bits of parchment from cultures past. But if we were to take sheaves and sheaves of ancient scriptural writing and put them through a gigantic press to squeeze the very essence of knowledge out of them – the insights that can truly help us make a difference in our lives every day and live by a code that's in tune with God's world – we'd come up with a few simple messages that the sages of our time have already neatly committed to bumper stickers.

>Have a nice day.
>Take it easy.
>Or, a fit-for-print version of my favorite: Life happens.

Because *life does simply happen.* And I believe there is no God that makes it happen *to us.* So perhaps the first step toward finding a God that really works is to adopt the notion of a God that doesn't do malicious things. I think it's okay to accept the idea that God doesn't actually do anything at all.

So where did our concept of a meddling, hands-on God come from? I think it stems from our universal desire to have some sort of super-parent who can direct our lives and be our protector, teacher and, well – our father. It's a concept to which we can all relate. We look to fathers to love us always, but also to scold us and discipline us when we need it. And, thanks to all the guilt we've built up around the whole concept of sin, we apparently need and want a lot of spanking. How many of us think it perfectly reasonable and normal that when we do something bad, our big Sky Dad will reach down and rap us on the knuckles? Or, worse, cast a scornful look our way and cause bad things to happen?

Instead, I choose to believe that there definitely is a God – at least some power that is greater than us – but not one who works like Not Me. I believe in a God who *is,* not one who *does.* Yes, God is all-loving or all-powerful, but God is also quite benign and passive. God didn't arbitrarily call my brother home early on a sunny summer morning in the prime of his life. An airplane broke. It's as simple as that.

I also believe that there is a lesson in everything that happens to us, and maybe that is the real reason why we experience joy and suffering in our lives. There is always some meaning – or gift – for us to receive, if we're willing to look for it or give it time to materialize, that will enrich our lives and add texture and meaning. Time and distance are the key elements that give us the clarity to see why events happen the way they do.

For years after 1988, I refused to believe that anything good could possibly emerge from the tragedy of my brother's death. I saw nothing but hurt and harm in all the loose ends of his needless death at such an early age, with so much promise laid out before him in life. But I can look back now and clearly see that something good did come out of it all. Each of us who knew him has learned and grown – through intense pain, as is often the case – as a result of his death. For me, casting aside what I believed about God opened the door to an entirely new way of thinking about religion and faith that brings immense joy, meaning and depth to my life. I'm not being selfish in acknowledging this – indeed, I did not ask for any of it to happen. But I realize and recognize that it did happen, and I am thankful for the lesson.

One Sunday morning several months after my brother's death, I decided to go to church, hoping for some momentary relief or maybe a tiny peck of resolution. I had been brought up to believe that church was where I would find God and that God either was the answer or at the very least knew the password to the secret door where the answers might be found. I was by myself on this occasion, and I drove to a church I had never attended and walked in after the service had started and took a seat in a rear pew. *Okay, God... I am ready.* Through the fog, I remember the preacher saying that *only in death do we achieve eternal life.* For whatever reason, that was all I heard him utter that dreary morning.

The thought made me anxious and uneasy. I was sick of death. Unwilling to be open minded through the pain of my loss, I stormed out noisily, letting the door slam behind me and vowing to never again darken the archways of that miserable place. Once again, the God whom I had known from childhood had failed me and left me wanting.

Only now, many years later, do I realize the significance of what I heard that day. I recognize, of course, that the preacher was giving a sermon on the prayer of Saint Francis. And what I mistakenly heard and understood as God demanding death as a payment for some mystical promise of eternity was in reality an instruction for me to cast off my old ways of thinking in order to learn something new – something powerful that would pave the way to an all-new spiritual world for me. Fate was telling me then that by allowing my old faith to die, I would receive a blank canvas on which to paint an entirely new vision of the way that God's power was supposed to work in my life.

I have not been disappointed by the work of art that continues to emerge on that canvas. I used the pain that I experienced in my life – like the pain we all experience at one time or another – to empower myself to shed the shallow beliefs and pat answers I had been fed up to that point and dig for something much deeper. Something that made sense – *a God that worked.*

I often think back to the lady who lost her son in church that afternoon, and I pray regularly that she has grasped a new understanding of God and lost the pain that I saw in her eyes. I hope she knows that God didn't single her – or her son or family – out for punishment. The Creator loved her, and loved her son – and even the man with the gun.

So who makes all of life's really rotten things occur or pulls the strings to make good things happen to one person and not another? Who is it that makes life so arbitrary?

Not God.

Three: Father Martin's Bell

When I was a boy growing up, my greatest ambition was to be the lead acolyte at the church where my family worshipped. I did pretty well in school and okay in Little League baseball, but the big red-carpeted space at the front of the expansive chapel was one place where I knew I could excel. I made it my goal to master all the myriad details – all the complex steps and procedures – required to pull off the Sunday morning service from the acolyte's bench beside the altar. I decided that I would set new standards for excellence in the Acolyte's Arts. I made it my life's goal to epitomize perfection in red and white robes.

My teacher in this endeavor was Father Harold Martin. He passed away many years ago, but was a very real and larger-than-life person to me at that point in my youth, so I have no problem whatsoever mentioning him here by name.

As an Episcopal priest, Father Martin was every bit God on Earth as far as I was concerned. He was a taskmaster, who held class every Sunday after the communion service for us fledgling altar boys, so that we could study and learn all the intricate minutiae required to prepare for, conduct and clean up after every type of Anglican service.

I started any given Sunday swinging from the ropes in the bell tower to signal the beginning of services. I lit the candles before each mass and put them out afterwards – all in a carefully defined order. I bore the cross up the aisle in the processional, carried the heavy books up and down the aisle for the readings, passed out plates for the offertory and generally helped to keep the show moving along in a quiet sort-of acolyte way.

After a short few years, I found myself in the position of Senior Acolyte, which afforded me a coveted post at the right side of the altar. Best of all, this new appointment gave me the responsibility of ringing Father Martin's special bell as he prepared the sacraments for Holy Communion. If you're familiar with the Episcopal brand of the Christian faith, you know that a communion service is often all about the "bells and the smells," referring to incense, chimes and other ceremonial embellishments. A full-blown Episcopal service can indeed be a beautiful thing, a very spiritually and emotionally uplifting event.

The ringing of Father Martin's bell was a carefully choreographed assignment. The bell itself was simple enough – it looked like a large salad bowl mounted upside down on a foot-high shaft attached to a pedestal. It was made of heavy, thick brass and was accompanied by a small mallet that looked like a judge's gavel. Striking the bell properly required a carefully placed glancing blow. Too dead-on and the bell yielded a bland clunking sound. But with the perfect blend of angle and force – sort of like the follow-through on a golf putt – the bell would produce a deep, mellow tone that could resonate for minutes on end. Mastering the bell itself was easy enough – until you added a few variables.

Variable number one was the script. Father Martin's special bell-driven mass involved ringing the bell at numerous specific spots throughout the preparation of the bread and wine before Holy Communion – the body and blood of Jesus Christ, to believers. At certain places in the service, he would either kneel or hold something high up over his head, and both of these motions required a ceremonial ding. One act called for a single ring, and the other called for a triple ring - although I can't remember which was for what. There was even one special bell-ringing move that involved a high-overhead hoist, a couple of kneels, and a big sprawled-out genuflection. *Ding, ding, ding, ding!*

All of Father Martin's special rings happened at multiple points throughout the thirty-minute run-up to the actual communion. And then there were several other odd and random rings scattered here and there throughout the service to accentuate some special phrase or other. To this day I can't remember it all – it was a regular ding-a-thon.

Variable number two was the fact that, as the lead acolyte and principal bell ringer, I had to kneel at the altar several steps below and to the right of Father Martin, and hunch over the bell as I rang it. That was all well and good, except that in order to ring the bell properly – with the right heavenly tone and at precisely the right time – I had to crane my neck outward and upward like a big turtle so that I could see his movements. And I had to do this while appearing to not look up for cues – I was, after all, kneeling in meditative prayer. It was an impossible act. After many years of giving it my very best effort, I never did truly master it.

To this day I can still see the image of God-like larger-than-life Father Martin looking down at me in my position behind and below with a look of disappointment. I can still see the subtle sideways shake of the head and the closing of the eyes. *Geez... when will you ever get it right?*

I share this story not to garner sympathy, but to illustrate the fact that for many years in my life growing up and trying to do all of the right things that God and religion asked of me, I never got past the idea that somehow I wasn't capable of measuring up in God's eyes. As a bell ringer, I was always a second off the mark, or off-center with the mallet, or in the wrong part of the program altogether. For me, Father Martin was God. Nobody ever bothered to tell me otherwise. And at a time in my young life when I needed to hear more than anything else that God loved me purely and simply – and how well I did or didn't ring that infernal bell didn't really matter – that signal was never given. Father Martin-God never said, *"That's okay, Jimmy. We'll get it next time."*

And I am not alone. There are plenty of us – hundreds of millions of us, or perhaps billions I would guess, of all faiths and denominations – who have grown up thinking that God was church. Or going to church. Or following a program or singing a hymn or wearing a robe or bringing a dish or writing a check or saying a prayer. Or ringing a bell. There exists a world of people from all walks of life and from every faith tradition who have bought into this idea – particularly during our younger years. Orthodox or Reformed. Catholic or Protestant. Christian, Jew, Muslim, Buddhist, Hindu or Pagan. Because of this, we've somehow grown up without realizing that religion – with all its manifestations of buildings and rituals and titles – is simply our best attempt to understand a concept that simply cannot be understood, or define an idea that truly defies definition. Religion, or church, is not God.

These days, I think that a church or other religious institution is, in a great many cases, the last place that many true seekers can find a meaningful spiritual connection.

In fairness, there are terrific and uplifting messages and events and functions and societies in nearly every house of worship – plenty to do to keep us busy with the business of religion. But as humans we invariably get caught up in the everyday trappings of faith and easily lose track of the spiritual fire that burns deep within the core of each of us. It's easy to confuse all the good feelings we can find at church – or temple, or mosque and so forth – with a deep and meaningful understanding of the Divine.

I am not a disbeliever in church or religion *per se*. In fact, quite the contrary. I honestly think that any organization that does so many good works and generally aims to keep such a large group of people focused on living positive, wholesome and healthy lives simply has to be worthwhile. Other than a few cults that have simply gone nuts and jumped over the edge of sanity and reason, all religious institutions are basically good. There is no arguing with the fact that many churches do an amazing and often unrecognized job of helping to promote better communities, health services, education and more. They give us foundation and structure in a world where we crave order. They feed the poor, nurse the sick, shelter the homeless and generally make God's Earth a better place to live.

I also do not presume to claim that people who belong to churches lack a true, deep and meaningful spiritual connection with God. Far from it. It is human nature for us to need some anchor on which to ground ourselves, to give our lives purpose and meaning and to give us a sense of belonging and identity. Church does that very well. Belonging to a church helps us to define who we are.

But I am saying that for many people – churchgoers or not – the quest for a God that truly works often goes straight through religion and off into a far bigger world of inquiry that lies in the undefined world beyond. We can use what we learn in church as a stepping-stone to follow our own lines of questioning and to clear the way for our own personal path to exploring and expanding our understanding of the world and our creator. We shouldn't stop at the bells. And we certainly shouldn't be held in check by the churches to which we belong. We shouldn't be limited by rituals and rites, or the very human criteria of all the well-meaning Father Martins we find in churches everywhere.

Virtually every religious group is keen to say that a church – any church – isn't a building at all, or bells or any other physical thing or place. A church, or at least a church family, is people – the living souls who breathe life into the bricks and mortar and keep the pews and coffers filled and do the usually wonderful things that religious congregations do. No doubt this is correct. But I think a red flag should be hoisted for those who easily get tied up in people and personalities that we can see, feel and hear – and mistakenly believe to be the manifestations of God in human form. We place tremendous faith in the people who run our churches, mosques, synagogues and so forth – much of it extremely well deserved.

But it's easy to forget that these men and women are our servants on our spiritual journey and not themselves the focus of our spiritual lives. It's natural to view someone with a title like "Father" as an authority figure. And it's normal to think of a "Pastor" – a term that stems from *pasture* – as a shepherd whose job it is to guide and guard a flock of helpless sheep from snarling wolves in the night. But humans are humans, and nothing more, and we should remember that all of these servants – no matter how wise and insightful – only learn real practical lessons as the rest of us do: through pain and experience and study and suffering. And by feeling free to ask questions – even difficult ones about the true meaning of God and faith. Like us, our clergy and other ministerial personages should always have more questions than answers.

These days I find it odd that many Roman Catholics hesitate not a second to visit a parish priest for marriage counseling or guidance on family issues. To me, that's a bit like going to a driving instructor who's never actually driven a car, or learning to fly from a pilot who's never left the ground. But when I think back to my upbringing and the conditioning I got from Father Martin – who stood before me wearing all those special robes and collars, speaking special words and phrases, incanting all those beautiful magic spells, all accompanied by the chimes of that mystical bell – I can clearly understand why we put so much faith and trust in the leaders who guide our churches and religious families.

I also find it mildly amusing these days that we search in so many ways and in so many places beyond bricks and mortar for physical manifestations of God that we can watch, touch and point to – we want to see something to help us believe. Over the past dozen years, we've seen Jesus in streaks on a windowpane and stains on the side of a building. We've seen the Virgin Mary in char marks on a grilled cheese sandwich. An acrylic protective structure was erected a few years ago in a largely Catholic part of my city to protect an image of the Virgin Mary that mystically appeared in a melted ice cream sandwich that had fallen from a vending machine. Globally, the grotto beneath the ancient chapel in Lourdes in France plays host to five million people each year – many hoping to find healing in the mystic waters. And more than five hundred examples of stigmata – statues that bleed or cry – have been reported in Catholic Europe over the past several centuries. We simply demand some way to touch, see, taste and hear the presence of God. We need some physical proof that will help us to believe.

Maybe it's just hitting middle age, or maybe it's being at this particular place on my spiritual journey, but I tickle myself these days thinking of what I might do if I suddenly discovered myself dressed in vestments and once again wielding the mallet to Father Martin's vaunted bell. I'm not rebellious by nature, and not one to typically go out of my way to cause a ruckus of any sort. But give me the opportunity now in the midst of all that ceremonious reverie, and I would likely ring with reckless abandon. And with each clang of the bell, I might ponder – internally or outloud, I don't know – *what is the purpose of this bell? Why is it so important that it peal so perfunctorily at such precise moments? How does it bring me closer to God? Who says we're not free to shake things up a bit and chime in ourselves on what God really means, or how God really works, or what we really need to do to explore the idea of God in our lives? Why do we have to be such conformists, doing the same things over and over again, century after century? Why did it take fifteen hundred years for the church to acknowledge that the Earth is not the center of the universe? Who among us claims to have a pure, perfect and complete understanding of the nature of God? Ding, ding, ding, ding!*

It's time that we all become bell ringers. A little out-of-sync bell ringing could be, on occasion, a pretty good thing throughout religion, I think. And there's no better time than now. Armed with a bell and mallet – maybe this book is my bell – I'm as ready as anyone to mount a bell-ringing crusade that will wake us up and jar our attention so that we can look lovingly but inquisitively at all the Father Martins of our lives and start asking *why* more often. If this crusade captures nobody else's attention or imagination, then at least it will have awakened mine.

My mother died of cancer in 2001, just five days after the horrific events of 9/11. She had been ill for a couple of years and fought with every ounce of strength to defeat the tumors that rapidly claimed her once-vigorous body. During those last months, we had ample opportunity to share much with each other, to ponder deep personal questions and to discuss our somewhat differing views on the nature of religion and spirituality – and God. One afternoon she launched into a fairly forceful discussion on my lack of official membership in a church congregation. At that time I was experimenting with many faith traditions, but didn't think of myself as overtly religious or tied to a specific way of believing. She pushed as only a mother can push. She demanded that I explain to her why I couldn't simply follow what my church of origin taught me and be happy with that and take my family and spend the rest of my life there and *move on happily ever after, amen!*

I told her as lovingly as possible that I found absolutely no problem with the faith of my upbringing. I thought it was wonderful for people who found their spiritual home there – especially her. But I needed more. In fact, I felt that my unique and personal relationship with the God that I knew demanded that I look beyond the church as I knew it to discover what might be found beyond. I explained to her that faith to me was not a destination but a journey – a spiritual voyage that I believed I would (or should) never complete. And, while I very much appreciated the kick-start I had received growing up in the church of my upbringing, I was now poking gently through the limits of what religion might teach to seek my own higher, clearer perspective of the true nature of the Divine. I explained to her that I hadn't rejected the church or recoiled away from it, but that I had simply shot through it and on to a broader realm of spiritual investigation.

Of course, she looked puzzled, as many people do when faced with a mild challenge to contemporary faith such as this. But I also noticed a change in her then – if not an acceptance of my personal faith journey, then maybe an understanding that I was at least on a path to somewhere. And that might be a good thing. She never again pushed me too firmly on that one issue, although she did gently nudge me on many others. We had an agreement from that point on that we both might be right – to some degree – about God and the afterlife and the nature of Divinity. We agreed that neither of us would truly know what came next until we experienced it for ourselves. And that was okay. She couldn't say it, but I think she approved of my quest. She knew it's what I had to do. And maybe there was a bit of seeker alive in her that wished me well on my journey.

My mother was a wonderful woman who did many great things in her life. But she had lived all of her years within the boundaries of the faith and religion she had been taught early on. Maybe she had asked the tough questions at a younger time, I don't know. But in the end she, like many who are rapidly approaching death, embraced her faith with an unyielding grasp. I thank her for the willingness to recognize that I had to move beyond the limits she knew to find a God that truly worked for me. I believe that she is now in whatever Heaven she envisioned.

As for Father Martin, I saw him several decades later, after I had moved away and then returned to the Mississippi Gulf coast as an adult on vacation. I was amazed at how small and insignificant he seemed. He was several decades older, of course, but also wilted and frail. He was no longer rector of the church but hung around like old priests do to assist with running the parish – or perhaps he showed up simply to intimidate the acolytes-in-training. I saw him in the sanctuary of the church, which also seemed strangely smaller than I remembered. I embraced him. I had forgiven him years earlier for not being able to laugh and smile with me as I clunked his bell off-cue. Or tell me that *God loved me anyway, no matter what* – a message that, in my view, represents the only words a child needs to hear in church. I realized that he, like everyone else, was a human much more than he was any type of God, and therefore prone to human failures and frailties. He, too, had been doing his best.

I also remember that before I shook his hand and left the church, I cast a glance up toward the altar. Father Martin's bell – like my youthful belief that he and his church were the Gods of my life – was gone.

Four: Dear God – You're Fired

I am an alcoholic and a drug addict. And I don't mind saying so. I am a person who, for many years in my life, washed handfuls of pills down with large quantities of alcohol and packed fairly large piles of strange powder up my nostrils in the misguided belief that those substances would somehow fix the problems that made up my world or at least would dull my senses enough so that I no longer cared about them. I have been in recovery – completely clean and sober – for nearly twenty years as of this writing. So most of the people who know me today wouldn't have a clue – or really care, for that matter – about the darker side of my history. We all go through seasons in our lives, some good and some not so good. The people with whom I work and interact in my life today know me for who I am now. And, to me, that is all that matters.

I got clean and sober through Alcoholics Anonymous. I understand that anonymity is a major tenet, indeed a spiritual foundation, of all twelve-step programs. But I also think the anonymity component of AA dates from an earlier time when to be known as a boozer or dope user could in fact be a true detriment to recovery. These days, I think the real purpose of anonymity rests in protecting others with whom I associate in recovery, and I will always do that. There are many doctors and airline pilots who truly need to remain anonymous. But as for me, I honestly think that nobody would think either more positively or negatively about me for sharing the lessons of my drinking and drug-using past. Really, it's a non-issue. And there you have it.

I mention it here only because my addiction and recovery have played a direct and powerful role in my discovery of a God that works. I'm not proselytizing for Alcoholics Anonymous or Narcotics Anonymous or the many other recovery groups that rely on the twelve steps. But I do want to highlight the fact that many millions of people who have never experienced any other form of spiritual connection have found one – and typically a very deep one – in recovery programs such as these.

I found a "Higher Power" in AA even though I wasn't looking for one. As I mentioned early on, losing my brother in such a tragic and sudden way back in 1988 sent me into a complete tailspin regarding faith, religion and God. I went through many profound changes during the following two years – readers who have lived through similar experiences will surely understand. But key among these was an absolute divorce from anything and everything I had come to know and believe about who God was and how that vengeful, demanding God worked in my daily life. God was simply not for me.

The fact is, by the time I got to the doors of AA in 1990, I harbored a true hostility toward God. Not only was

I a "non-believer" or atheist or what have you, I had a genuine hatred for the God that had taken my brother *for want of a new piece of statuary in His Great Garden in the Sky.* The miracle of recovery programs like AA – and again, my mission here is not to promote anything – is that the program can have a lot of patience with hardheads like me. As described in the popular poem *Footsteps in the Sand,* I have learned in retrospect that God – or whatever my clearly ambiguous understanding of a Higher Power is today – was hard at work in my life a long time before I was consciously ready or willing to take any bold spiritual steps on my own. God was carrying me when I could not carry myself during my tenuous and wobbly early days and months in sobriety.

I not only didn't like God, or want God in my life, I loathed God – the entire concept. And this, of course, flies at odds with all of the basic ideas of twelve-step recovery. Or does it? It is perhaps well known that the key to coming clean from booze and drugs rests with learning to believe that there is something greater than ourselves at work in the world that can take control of our mismanaged lives and keep us free from selfish distractions and focused on finding serenity and purpose in the world around us. This has certainly happened in my life – for the most part.

But the way this works isn't by forcing some pre-defined idea of God down anybody's throat. In fact, you can find very little – almost nothing at all – in the way of a definition of God in any literature or dogma espoused by any twelve-step recovery program. The big idea is that each and every one of us must come to find a God *as we understand Him.* We each are challenged to launch out on a spiritual journey to find a connection to the Divine that can show us how to live and learn in ways that we couldn't before. In short, we are each encouraged to find a unique and personal God that works.

Without giving away the secret handshake, I can tell you that twelve-step meetings typically involve a prayer or two. It's not uncommon to end a meeting with everyone in the group standing in a circle and saying the Lord's Prayer or the Serenity Prayer. Chances are, you've seen at least that much on the odd documentary or perhaps in a movie or two. Even more likely, you've come into contact with some of the basic ideas of AA through a friend or family member. There are prayers throughout the AA program, including several that coincide with specific steps – like the 3rd Step, where we surrender our will and our life over to the care of God as we understood Him, or the 7th Step, where we ask our Higher Power to take away the character defects that keep pulling us back into old behaviors. There are others, but those are the major prayer stops along the path. Indeed, the entire process of twelve-step recovery is designed to create a very subtle, yet highly profound, spiritual epiphany. Step Twelve refers to a "spiritual awakening as the result of" all the prior steps.

There are many who would say that recovery from addiction based on spiritual connection to a vaguely defined Higher Power doesn't work. That's fine – AA takes no position on that and neither will I. Each person is free to find what works best. Again, I'm not here to push one road to God over another. But I will say that I believe the early developers of twelve-step recovery did an amazing job of bringing together all of the universal spiritual truths that can be drawn from virtually every faith tradition and boiling them down in one very large kettle to yield the very essence of what we need to know and do in our daily lives to live successfully by any measure. I honestly believe that efforts like this have been divinely inspired – there is no doubt in my mind. And there are millions and millions of recovering drunks and addicts like me around the world today who would quickly and adamantly agree.

But the whole God thing wasn't easy for me in the beginning. It was impossible, really. I walked through the doors of AA back in 1990 looking for a way to get my life back on track, not to seek spiritual growth. I had a two-year-old daughter, a failing marriage, a miserable day-to-day existence and no real outlook for a happy future. I drank and used drugs every day to try to dull the pain in my life – yet drugs and alcohol had long since stopped working. I didn't want to die, but I wasn't all that sure I had much of a desire to live, either – at least not in the manner I was living at the time. Each day was a twenty-four-hour span of time to be endured, not a celebration of God's world to be enjoyed from beginning to end, as it largely is today. I have succeeded in AA – for nearly two decades, one day at a time – in spite of myself. And all because of the concept of God as I understand Him.

Here's how it worked for me. A man I had come to know around the AA meeting hall and had grown to respect had made note of the fact that I avoided God. When others stood to recite a prayer at the end of meetings, I would stand and hold hands silently. I also avoided the subject of God or a Higher Power during open discussions – when called upon, I would change the subject. But here is a good thing about most twelve-step groups: they are filled with folks who, like me, also walk through the door recovering from religion. This man, whose name was Robert (in what I find a terrific irony, I never knew his last name), was one such person. And he knew exactly how to help me get over the God hurdle.

Robert invited me out for coffee after a meeting one night and brought up the subject of God. As if on cue, I launched into a well-rehearsed diatribe about what a lousy idea God was, and how that nasty old white-bearded Divine Terrorist purposely had it out to get me and wreck my life and cause all of these miserable things to happen and then not be there for me when I needed Him most. I rambled on and on exactly the way I often hear other newcomers vent these days. As I droned, Robert sat patiently, nodding occasionally, waiting for me to finish. When I was done, he simply said, "It sounds like you need to fire that God and maybe find a new one."

I sat in stunned silence.

What? You mean I can do that?

"Sure," he said. "If the God you know works the way you just described, then it's perfectly okay to give him the boot and hire a new one – I would – and then find one that makes sense to you." I was dumbfounded. It wasn't so much the simplicity of the idea that took me by surprise – all really good ideas are simple – but the notion that we could so freely discuss a concept that I held to be so sacrosanct. To me, God was the Almighty, the all-powerful One, the Man – Creator of Heaven and Earth. And to talk about Him as if I were a human resources director looking to replace one shop floor supervisor with another… it all seemed so novel… and intriguing…and dangerous. Father Martin would surely never approve of this. I waited for a lightning bolt – which never came.

Robert went on to describe the process that I should use to go about finding and hiring a new God – one that would work for me and keep me sane, secure and serene. I should get out a blank sheet of paper and write out a job description – a list of requirements and qualifications for the job. I should completely define the God that I could and would use to guide me through the rest of my life – with all of my foibles and failures, warts and all. It sounded simple enough.

The more I thought about this idea, the more energized I became. I wanted a God that had, above all, a sense of humor. I needed laughter in my life. I wanted a God that would accept me completely as I was, and understand that my innermost desire to be a good husband, father and human didn't always reveal itself in my outward actions. I wanted a God who wouldn't sit as Lord over me with that damned ledger keeping track of everything that I did – right or wrong, good or bad – but instead would look deep into my heart to know that I am generally a good and decent person. And I wanted a God that was at least somewhat predictable – even if that meant being predictably unpredictable. This meant a God that didn't randomly do things to me, or to others or the world around me. Life was messy and cluttered up enough on its own.

The end result of the process that started that evening was an entirely new way of thinking about the idea of God – a seed tossed into fertile soil. I couldn't yet begin the task of defining what my new God would be – I'm still working on that today. But at least I could go out into the world with the clear understanding that God wasn't responsible for all the challenges, difficulties and losses that had come my way – or those that would inevitably come my way in the years ahead. I could stop blaming God for the rotten things that happened in the world around me. And I could stop playing the role of victim at the same time. You can see how hope began to immediately spring from this – for me – revolutionary new idea.

Over the next weeks and months, I launched into an incredible new world of reading and learning – of exploring with eyes wide open. Still generally morbid and morose in my overall attitude some three years after my brother's tragic accident, a friend gave me a copy of Harold Kushner's *When Bad Things Happen to Good People* – an amazing book that appeared as a godsend exactly when it was supposed to. I do believe the old adage that when the pupil is ready the teacher will appear. In this case, Kushner laid out the idea – and why are these things so simple after you've learned them? – that God isn't somebody who sits opposite me at the big Table of

Life, but rather someone who is my friend and our ally when times get tough. It was no longer Me vs. God, but God and I vs. whatever might come my way. This was a marvelous and wide-open new concept to me.

So by defining and hiring – with sign-on bonus – a God who would forever sit on my side of the table and team with me as we faced life's challenges together, I could finally, once and for all, dismiss the question: God, who's side are you on? I would never, ever be alone again. How marvelous. I should mention that one of the many requirements I placed on the God that I hired then was that this new benefactor be continuously amorphous. I knew enough to know that my life had changed dramatically many times since my youth, and would continue to change as I grew – perhaps even at a more rapid pace than before. The God that I know and rely upon in my life today does exactly that. We change, we grow, we learn together. Each new challenge brings with it an opportunity for growth, often through pain. But that's the way life is. And I'm very much okay with that.

With this new thinking about God, I find that I generally feel in sync, relaxed and peaceful in the world around me. I am largely insignificant – ironically, I feel quite anonymous – in the grand scheme of things, which suits me just fine. Nobody picks me out for life's big calamities. As my favorite scriptural bumper sticker so eloquently says, *Life Happens* – and I get to learn and grow. It's as simple as that. God as I understand Him and I get to experience it all together.

I shared some of this experience with my mother a couple of years before she died, around the time that she first learned of her cancer. She scolded me as only a loving mother can on the dangers of creating my own God. *There is one God and only one God,* she explained, and *He is revealed to us through Holy Scripture.* For me to stray off on my own was heresy. She believed this because she needed to – and because I think that way of believing worked for her. This point of differentiation between us was the launching pad for a long and wonderful dialog we had on spiritual matters that lasted right up to the time of her death.

For me, my mother's God wasn't a good fit. He had either stopped working or had never worked at all. I needed something more. And I owe my life today – generally a happy, healthy and fulfilling life – to my new understanding of a God that continues to be revealed in greater detail each day. In fact, the new relationship I have with an altogether different sort of God today has enabled me to take a completely fresh look at things I've known, thought, said and believed about God my entire life. An example? *The Lord's Prayer.*

To me, in the days and months following my brother's accident, the Lord's Prayer came to epitomize everything that I knew – and ultimately distrusted – about religion. In many ways, a prayer as ubiquitous as the Lord's Prayer can actually become the face of the church or religion or God – it is, to many – for it seems to be one of those things that finds its way into ceremonies and rites that extend far beyond church walls. Although primarily a Christian prayer drawn from Jesus' Sermon on the Mount, it is voiced routinely by persons of all faiths. Ironically, to me anyway, the Lord's Prayer is common within the rooms of Alcoholics Anonymous – spaces that become the spiritual home to many who are recovering not only from drugs and alcohol but from religion, too. In my early years in recovery, I sometimes wondered why this was. But always fell back on the idea that the Lord's Prayer is a kind of a universal something-to-say when nothing else seems appropriate, and left it at that. The spiritual foundation of AA is built upon a basic set of cornerstone principles – big ideas boiled down to simple forms. There is nothing new or revolutionary about any of these, for they are timeless spiritual concepts that are common to all faiths.

Gems like:

> *One day at a time.*
> *Easy does it.*
> *Surrender to win.*
> *First things first.*
> *Keep your side of the street clean.*

I had come to know and believe in these rugged axioms, having been shown through the real-life example of my own recovery that these simple gems of truth could and would help me to live a quiet, steady and spiritual life. I remember at first seeing these serendipitous lines and thinking that they would look right at home on embroidered pillows in some grandmother's living room or on wall posters next to fuzzy photos of daisies and little kittens. But a universal truth becomes a universal truth by proving itself to be useful, and these and many other easy rules to live by have earned their way rightfully into the everyday world of recovery by delivering fruitful results.

And so one day, quite by accident, as I was listening to the Lord's Prayer, I began to hear new words and new ideas. I wasn't into the idea of a father-god just then, but I could relate to some power greater than myself. "Give us this day our daily bread" suddenly became *one day at a time.* "Thy will be done" transformed itself easily, too – becoming a reminder that I must *surrender my life to something other than myself every day.* And "Forgive us our trespasses as we forgive others" suddenly looked glaringly like a reminder to focus on my actions and make amends wherever and whenever necessary, remembering not to dwell on the actions of others – in other words, to *keep my side of the street clean.* Of course, "Deliver us from evil" became a mantra for avoiding drugs and alcohol and other things that might cause me harm. In fact, virtually every word of the

Lord's Prayer now took on a bigger and broader meaning for me. By looking more deeply at the underlying meanings of the words, I was able to see that – archaic language aside – the prayer is in fact quite timeless and relevant.

Set apart from the marbled walls of church buildings or the illuminated parchments of medieval manuscripts, here is how I view the meaning of the prayer today:

Our Father, who art in heaven,
Hallowed be thy name.

> *Immense and unknown power that created us, I acknowledge your presence. I am not here by accident.*

Thy Kingdom come,
Thy will be done,
On earth as it is in heaven

> *I do not understand the way the universe works, but accept that what happens is what happens. There is some greater purpose.*

Give us this day our daily bread.

> *I trust that I will have everything I need to survive and thrive in this world today. Life is good. I must live by faith, not fear.*

And forgive us our trespasses,
As we forgive those who trespass against us.

> *Help me to live a positive life, not harming other creatures or the world around me. Help me to recognize that the world and its people may seem*

> *imperfect. Help me to make amends when needed and leave fewer messes than I create.*

And lead us not into temptation,
But deliver us from evil.

> *Give me the strength to stay away from things that are bad for me – with the help of a power greater than myself, I can be safe, sober, sane and serene. Help me to become a better person.*

For thine is the kingdom, the power and the glory
For ever and ever. Amen

> *God is the force that drives my life, and for this I am grateful. So be it.*

By redefining the way that my God and I communicate through this basic prayer, I am convinced that I have not changed the nature of God in any way. I have simply made the force that works for me more understandable, more relevant. Like all good employee/employer relationships, we have cleaned up our lines of communication so that we can operate more efficiently, with far fewer opportunities for misunderstanding or bungled assignments. We each know and comprehend our roles, and we know that we depend upon each other to succeed. And this process of continual reassessment and evaluation has extended itself into other areas of our working relationship, too. After all, we are on a common quest for greater productivity in the endeavors that mean the very most to me in the enterprise of my life.

My addictions put me in a place where I was forced to learn and grow… or die. Robert, who long ago moved off and still remains anonymous to me, provided the tools I needed to fire a deadbeat boss that was grinding me down.

I used an all-new set of tools to learn what God was *not* and establish some much clearer lines of communication. By laying this foundation for a new relationship with God, I opened up a marvelous new door of discovery that continues to help me learn all that God *can be*.

Five: Jerry's Perfect Pets

I spent the early years in recovery from drug and alcohol addiction on an amazing quest for spiritual knowledge. With my eyes now opened to a world of new possibilities – and an abundance of fresh energy as a result of healthy living – I set out to read and learn as much as I could. My mind was filled with questions galore. You never really realize how deep a hole can be until you start to fill it up.

By this time, I had worked my way into the position of Creative Director at one of the city's leading ad agencies. I had notched some spectacular successes during the early years of my career – far more by luck than by talent. I had gathered up my share of shiny trophies at black-tie events in New York and elsewhere, and the momentum of my reputation as a clever thinker and solid presenter had carried me forward through the juvenile days when my performance had quite obviously begun to suffer as a result of ever-increasing drug and alcohol abuse. Career velocity can be a very good thing. I had, in fact, been taken under the wings of several older "admen" whose unwavering support I will always appreciate. Most hardcore users and drinkers I have known are – almost without exception – above-average thinkers and gifted performers when the pressure is on. Not surprisingly, many conventional old "admen" are notoriously heavy drinkers.

One of my most ironic memories from this period springs from an assignment I received to develop a broad-sweeping drug-free workforce campaign that the Federal government wanted to make available to businesses nationwide. On the appointed morning, I presented my concept to a roomful of high-level bureaucratic types from a smorgasbord of government agencies – high as a kite the whole time. The campaign received thunderous applause and was accepted with hardly a challenge – a response that I relished immensely. I still get tickled when I run across the certificate I received – signed by the president. I also wonder if perhaps my fogged and clouded state lent the breakthrough insights that gave the campaign its depth and meaning. I'll never know.

In those delicate and nascent early days of sobriety, my office was situated next to a major mall, and I would take almost daily opportunities during lunch to stroll over and wander up and down looking at windows and people and venturing into the various shops. I had found new color in life – sobriety had created the effect in me of wearing polarized lenses for the first time in many years. Colors were brighter, sounds were louder and tastes were sharper. Maybe this was a continuation of the idea that when the pupil is ready the teacher appears. I was very clearly a willing and eager student. I wanted to absorb as much of life as I possibly could to make up for the several precious years I felt I had lost.

One of my favorite stops during most mall tours was a wonderful place called Jerry's Perfect Pets. It was a large pet store – with all sorts of dogs and cats and lizards and birds occupying most of the front portion of the shop. But the rear part was completely devoted to one of the largest collections of fish I have ever beheld. It was apparent to anyone that Jerry – whoever he was – had a real thing for fish. He sold animals with fur and feathers because you can't have a pet store and not do that. But fish – especially reef fish of the saltwater variety – were his obvious passion. The back of Jerry's Perfect Pets was made up of row upon row of large and wonderful tanks of virtually every kind of exotic fish imaginable.

I would often spend thirty to forty-five minutes in this section of the store each day at lunch, walking up and down the rows and marveling at the amazing creatures. One of my favorite tanks held an awesome assortment of corals, all covered with brightly colored living organisms of various types, sizes and shapes. Sea cucumbers, sponges, anemones, urchins, things hard and things soft… the tank was filled to the brim with an amazing selection of sea life. In fact, you could stare at that tank for hours and still not see everything there was to see. Often, you would only spot a living thing by *not* looking for it – so clever and delicate was the ornate and intricate camouflage that protected all the wonderful little nautical organisms.

All of which – in an unplanned and roundabout way – set the stage for the enlightenment that was to quickly follow.

Working in advertising, I spent years rubbing elbows every day with a host of genuinely gifted and talented designers, illustrators and artists. We created truly beautiful annual reports, ads and brochures, the kind that made clients sit back and say *Ahhh!* We prided ourselves on being a wellspring of creative thinking, clever witticisms and brilliant aesthetics. We were the very best at what we did and certainly on a par with any pool of talent you would find in any of the world's leading design Meccas. Madison Avenue had nothing on us.

But no one with whom I had ever worked could have come up with the amazing beauty that I saw before me in those tanks at Jerry's Perfect Pets. Nobody.

I saw delicate little shrimp, amazing in every tiny detail, artfully painted in brilliant bands of crimson and white. I saw fish in odd and perplexing shapes, painted in mosaics of stripes, plaids and paisleys – all blended together. I saw combinations of forms and colors that no designer would ever normally use. I saw vibrant and conflicting colors arranged side-by-side and atop each other that simply didn't make any sense – purples and oranges next to bright pinks. And yet they were incredible and beautiful and functional. I saw shapes and colors and sizes and forms that Peter Maxx, Andy Warhol or other designers from the heyday of psychedelics couldn't have created with an unlimited supply of the world's best acid. What I saw could simply never have been man-made at all.

So there, amid the sea life at Jerry's Perfect Pets, the door opened up for me to the idea that there must be some amazing and incredible power greater than any of us that caused all of this to be. A picture says a thousand words. And for the first time, I envisioned a God that I could not only understand, but one that I could also embrace and with whom I could build a strong and lasting relationship. The fish and other living things in those tanks would be my launching pad to a marvelous new world of spiritual discovery.

Several years ago, my wife and I spent a quiet afternoon at a nature preserve hidden high up in the mountains of central Costa Rica. This park held a massive and wonderful butterfly farm – a football field-sized enclosure where butterflies of all shapes and sizes grew and fluttered freely – often landing on the noses and fingertips of smiling visitors.

As I am prone to do in such places, I wandered off on my own, gawking in amazement at the beauty and mystery of the natural world. After some time, I found myself off in a quiet corner separated from the large open area in a space where workers in lab coats scurried about examining walls covered with shelves of tiny cocoons – each a delicate chrysalis – in various states of metamorphosis. I looked more closely and found the small, hanging pods in shapes that looked for all the world exactly like the bark of the trees on which they hung, or precisely like the leaves with which they shared their branches. So perfect is the art of the living world.

As I eventually turned to leave, I found myself standing next to a small rack of shiny silver earrings. *Ah, the place wouldn't be complete without a souvenir stand,* I thought. But when I looked more closely, I saw one of the chrome-plated earrings begin to stir – first with a tiny shake and then a more pronounced wobble – until it gently opened up to reveal the delicate, moist and shapeless forms of wings which emerged to dry gently in the cool mountain air. I stared in amazement as this marvel unfolded before my unblinking eyes. Surely no master artisan whom we are able to comprehend is behind a work of art such as this.

Over the past decade or so, much noise has come from folks who want to advance the agenda of "Intelligent Design." I think they perhaps started with the right idea – the same notion that I gained staring at the wonders at Jerry's Perfect Pets or the magic of the butterfly nursery that there simply has to be a divine spark behind the world we know. We are in perfect agreement on that much. But the thin veneer of pseudo-science quickly peels back to reveal that the divine creator touted by Intelligent Design promoters is simply the God of Genesis wearing a lab coat. How sad that they have the right idea but won't let it shine forth in all its own beauty and mystery without snarling it all up in tired old ideas of creationism.

There is tremendous fear associated with changing long-established and traditional ways of thinking. All change involves fear – fear of the unknown, of unpredictable outcomes, of having to establish new rules of understanding about our lives and the world around us. For creationists and other dogmatic religious types, it seems impossible to accept the idea that we don't need to know the specifics of the Master Designer. We don't have to understand or explain anything. We simply must accept that it is what it is – and it is perfect exactly that way.

I have a theory. I believe that man created God and not the other way around – or at least the *idea* of God that we commonly share. And I have a postulate that proves it, at least to me. Here it goes: If God created us – indeed, made us in His image and revealed Himself to us through various scriptures – then why does God come in so many shapes and forms and identities in different cultures all around the globe? Why is the God of the various monotheistic religions so different between faiths? Why would God be so different even within a specific religion? If there is one true God, then surely He – or She, or It – would make sure that we all caught a glimpse of the same divine ID card. We would all know and believe the very same things. *Undeniably.* And we don't.

The farther I go down the spiritual path that has become my life, the more I realize that nobody truly knows the nature of the Divine. The more questions we think we answer, the more questions we, in fact, generate. For believers who grew up hearing every Sunday that God created the earth in six days – with a day-by-day rundown of accomplishments – then rested on the seventh, interjecting the notion that there may be other possible approaches is a bit like shaking up the glass snow globe that goes out on the end table at Christmas. It's unsettling.

I'll state again that I'm no expert at anything relating to faith or religion – just a guy who's experienced quite a bit down on the working end of life. I'm also no scientist, so I dare not speak authoritatively on a subject like evolution. But I am a common sense kind of person who, if anything, hasn't been afraid to peel back the covers to look at life through clear and reasoned eyes. People of either camp who espouse the idea that it's "my way or no way at all" miss the opportunity to look at all the subtle points of view in between that can shed light on bigger, better, broader thinking. Literal creationists like to paint a picture of evolution as something completely random. I listen to them in complete astonishment on the radio all the time as I scan through the many religious stations in my area. *If it didn't happen like it says in the Bible, then it must have happened completely by accident, and without any sort of form or reason, right?* Of course not. This "either/or" thinking truly misses the point that of course there has been some grander brushstroke at work behind the masterpiece of our natural world. It's simply who or what did the painting that's the point of contention.

As the debate continues in states like Kansas and Pennsylvania – and now Texas – over whether or not to teach the science of evolution (it's not a theory, any more than God is theoretical) I have seen statistics presented in the media that should give us all cause for pause. One study showed that nearly half of all Americans believe in literal creationism as described in the opening book of the Bible – this, in a nation that pioneered virtually every one of the top one hundred innovations of the past century. People believe this because it's what they've been taught from birth onward, and because they have also been taught that to doubt religious concepts in any way is to defy God and risk being condemned to a theoretical lake of fire. Something clearly has to change. And because religion *can't* change – to do so would be a blatant admission that the teachings of thousands of years might be wrong or at the very least incomplete – it is we on the receiving end of faith who must be willing to look at age-old beliefs in a new light and through fresh lenses and put a final stop to the either/or thinking of literal creationism.

I often think back to my introduction to Hans Christian Andersen's *The Emperor's New Clothes* in high school literature. Written as a fairy tale for children in 1837, the story – like much of the work of Dr. Seuss a century later – was aimed squarely at adults and satirically highlighted the farcical ways that we adhere to conformity – how eagerly we go along with the beliefs of the masses. The story surely has huge ramifications in our recent world of politics, but it has also always held great meaning for me in the religious realm. As we are presented with more and more evidence of the ways the natural world has evolved in all the glory of God's master plan, the time must soon come for the larger group of us to stand and boldly announce that age-old religious views of the ways in which the world came to be and operates today are simply naked. We no longer need to pretend that we can see the teachings of the ancient faiths dressed up in the splendor and colors of amazing fabrics and gilded patterns. Instead we can follow the blissful honesty of a single small voice that calls it like it is – *pure creationism is simply wearing no clothes,* at least in the literal sense. By doing so, we level the playing field of learning, so that we can fully open the gates to understanding the majesty and wonder of God's creation.

I speculate that the vast majority of people who miss no opportunity to take potshots at Charles Darwin for the theories he outlined in *On the Origin of Species* have never been to the Galapagos Islands to see what he saw a century and a half ago. I made the trip a few years back and spent ten of the most amazing days of my life there, covering a mere fraction of the beauty and grandeur of that fascinating place. It's pretty hard to discount what we see with our own eyes. And I witnessed for myself a small part of what Darwin saw: tortoises of the same genetic species who have changed and evolved physically over a relatively brief period of time to meet the differing demands for food and survival on the archipelago's various islands. Or the finches whose beaks have lengthened or shortened to better catch insects on the varying trees of the different islands. One can see real evidence of evolution everywhere in this wonderful living laboratory: in the birds, the plant life and – in the most incredible ways – in the life under the sea. For a fish-lover like me, an afternoon spent snorkeling in the Galapagos is like Jerry's Perfect Pets on steroids.

I took away two very clear lessons from the Galapagos – the Enchanted Islands – that don't conflict in any way. First, there definitely has to be some Divine Creator. Nothing that we could ever conceive, comprehend or create ourselves can produce the amazing works of beauty and art that we see in the natural world around us. And second, there is a very beautiful randomness in all of God's creation. Everything does change, often unpredictably – but only within the context of a brilliantly conceived master plan. In fact, part of the beauty of creation itself is the very randomness that creationists tend to decry. You see, we *can* have it both ways.

But humans are understandably unhappy to live in a world without hard and fast answers. It's not good enough for us to simply accept and revel in the beautiful chaos that surrounds us. It's better for us – easier for us – if we have answers. And conventional religion provides at least one such answer, however out-of-sync it may be with the physical world we inhabit. It provides something to hold on to, so that we don't have to ask hard questions or feel the uncertainty and fear that come with change.

During the final two dark years when I was drinking and using drugs every day to try to retreat from the seemingly nonstop change that was overwhelming me in my life

– the sudden death of a loved one, the birth of my daughter, the pressures of a new job, the dread of having to behave like an adult in a grown-up world when every part of me wanted to flee back to the innocence of childhood – I did everything in my power to stop the inevitable flux that came my way. I had not yet realized that all change brings newness. And this freshness – whether positive or negative – is the real narcotic of life that adds zest and feeling and depth to living. I have known many people over the years who seem frozen in time – unwilling or unable to face the uncertainty that hides behind a closed door in front of them. They seem convinced that *the devil we know is far preferable to the devil we don't.* Their lives may be miserable – as mine once was – but they are too hesitant or afraid to let go of one way of believing in God to discover the unknown possibilities of defining and developing a new one that might make more sense.

I have heard that there is a tribe deep in the jungles of the Amazon basin that hunts a certain type of monkey for food. Knowing that these monkeys are drawn to a specific variety of nut that grows in the forest, the tribesmen place one of these nuts inside a heavy clay jar that has a neck just big enough to accommodate the nut and nothing else. They place these jugs in the clearings at night, knowing that the monkeys will use their tiny hands to try to grab the nuts and draw them out. Unable to do so, the hapless primates remain firmly attached to the jugs – their grip on the nuts unyielding – until the hunters gather them up the following morning.

As humans, we are like that; we hold on desperately to an old idea or an outdated way of thinking about how we should live our spiritual lives – or explore our connection to the God that empowers us – and allow ourselves to be devoured by our inability to change and grow. We become stunted and stale. We believe that we have come to know everything there is to know about God – or we are told as much by parents and pastors – and we simply stop looking, exploring and asking if there might be more that we don't understand. We give up and simply accept ideas that we may not truly believe – because we're supposed to. We are forbidden to rock the boat, even if doing so frees us from a spiritual sandbar and enables us to drift off with the tides toward greater understanding.

Instead of fleeing into the dark night at the prospect of unpredictable change like I once did, I now choose to think of each day as an all-you-can-eat buffet. There are many things that I will like, but also a few things that I won't. There are certain to be a few surprises – a helping or two of things that I've never tried but might enjoy. Today I relish the idea of change and gladly accept the fact that in order for me to grow and achieve the fullness of life that I know my God wants for me, I simply must be receptive to constant change. For it is inevitable. I know that every day that I'm blessed enough to rise from my bed, something or someone will enter my life that I did not expect the day before. What gifts! And I simply refuse to believe that I know the final answers to anything – instead welcoming with open arms the change and growth and the unexpected surprises that lie ahead of me continually on my faith journey.

Darwin was one brave fellow, in my humble opinion. He was not afraid of change. A deeply religious man, he spent the balance of his life working to reconcile the physical world he studied with the metaphysical faith he practiced. Surely it was much more difficult for him to launch his ideas on evolution back in the mid-1800s than it is for me to yammer on about a new way of thinking about God in this day and age. His challenge of the established order came at a time when Nicolaus Copernicus was still considered a heretic in some parts of the world for suggesting that the Earth was not the center of the Universe. But Darwin's presentation of evidence has made significant changes in the way we understand God's living world around us – changes that in my mind do not conflict in any way with the notion that we are all here by some divine order. Darwin's work opened a door to new ways of thinking about old religious ideas. And that's a small – or perhaps large – reason why we can be free to think differently about God in today's world. And come ever closer to finding a God that works.

Just a few years after I had my life-changing experience at Jerry's Perfect Pets, the store went out of business. Maybe Jerry was much better at understanding fish than he was at running a retail shop – I deeply regret that. Or maybe he moved off to a beach somewhere to be within a short snorkel of the reefs and fish he clearly loved so much – in which case I envy him greatly. Either way, I think Jerry was successful beyond belief at understanding and appreciating the beauty of the natural world around us. He had an obvious passion, and he followed it. Along the way, he and his marvelous fish helped to open the door to a bigger, brighter, better spiritual world for me, and perhaps many others.

Thank you, Jerry. Wherever you are.

Six: Of Deities and Dumpsters

Somewhere, back in the dark corner of an alley in some God-forsaken, run-down and desolate urban ghetto, a homeless person curled up behind a dumpster and died last night. I don't know who or where specifically, but I take it on faith that if I searched the newspaper of any given major city in this country, I'd find a story something like that. Then again, maybe not – stories about the tragic deaths of some of our less fortunate brethren seldom see the light of day. But if we checked the coroners' offices, or the morgues, I bet we'd find what we're after for this analogy: somewhere, somebody who wouldn't have garnered much of our attention in daily life fell asleep cold and hungry in the dark last night, and quietly moved from this life and on into the next.

And that person, in the first instant – *the very first nanosecond* – of death, came to know more about the true nature of the afterlife and divinity than Billy Graham and the Pope put together. Infinitely more. In true reality, that person learned more in the first microsecond of death about what comes next than all of the noted religious authorities of all faiths combined, from all time. All the pastors, all the imams, all the priests and cardinals, all the monks and yogis and gurus – more than everyone with every doctoral degree in divinity who has ever lived.

And the point I wish to make is this: nobody knows more about the true nature of God than you already do yourself. You have the power, in your own mind, with your own questions, your own instincts, and your own intuition, to do as good a job as anybody at coming up with an understanding of who or what God truly is. You have as much ability in the gray matter that fills your cranium to define God – and how we should live our lives according to the laws of that Great Spirit – as any authority who has ever tackled the subject. You have everything you need in your own reasoning abilities to understand the real nature of life, of God, and of what may or may not await us beyond this Earthly existence.

That is because, despite the teachings of nearly all of the sacred texts, everything we think we know about God comes not directly from God, but from us. From mere mortals – humans like you and me. There is much discussion these days about who actually wrote the Bible, or its many various books. Experts, both secular and religious, generally agree that there may have been four or more main authors, or editors, who pulled the work together over the course of fifteen hundred years or more. This library of books has subsequently been passed through dozens of major editorial boards and revised, translated and updated over many more centuries to give us the Bible that we hold aloft today. Or actually the *series* of Bibles we hold aloft today, for there are many different iterations – more than five thousand versions, I read recently. I can't speak for others, but as a child I pretty much got the general impression that God himself had given us these sacred words. And I do mean literally. Didn't Moses sit down and scribble out the first five books – *the Pentateuch* – as his divine boss dictated from above?

Truth is, it doesn't take much effort as a religious consumer to find the mark of human hands all over the history and universal understanding of faith. From start to finish. Completely. One hundred percent. And, of course, those human hands have been wielded with a full suite of human motives – greed, love, domination, compassion, control, curiosity, power and more.

Does this take any steam out of the value of works like the Bible? Of course not. The Bible, the Tanakh (the sacred book of Judaism), the Koran and all major religious texts we use in the world today have great and fantastic bits of wonderful and useful knowledge for living, giving and loving in this life. This is because a universal truth is a universal truth, regardless of its origination. A good snippet of advice is grand to have, whether it comes from a teacher, a parent, a friend or Aunt Edna. Nearly all of religion has great things to teach us. Learning and studying about religion can expose us to the hard-earned experience and knowledge of a thousand generations that have come and gone before. And who wouldn't want to take advantage of that?

Of course, there are a few bits of wisdom that have lost their luster and usefulness over the years. Modern-day preachers don't spend much time going over all the Mosaic laws as outlined in books like Leviticus and Deuteronomy. But if you ever need good guidelines on how to measure a grain harvest or advice on how to discipline your slaves or sell your daughter, those books provide a wealth of great and useful information.

So have the Billy Grahams and Popes of the world intentionally set themselves up to be God's right-hand men, ecumenical CEOs with direct hotlines to the Heavenly

Father? I think not. I think that we, as curious humans, have done that for them. Or maybe *to* them. Because we have a natural and insatiable desire to know what's behind the curtain, we look to anyone or anything that offers the promise of an answer as the most likely authority. I can't help but imagine that when Billy Graham or the Pope stare into the mirror as they shave each morning, they have to wonder – as we all do – what the real answers might be. And I think they each know, like the unfortunate fellow who died last night has already discovered, that we will only truly understand when the time comes for us to each make the transition for ourselves. These men may have unquestioning belief, but they must have some small iota of doubt, too. Belief and doubt must go together – they complement each other – and we can never have one without its opposite.

So while some traditionalists think it a sacrilege to divulge that Mother Teresa struggled with the true nature of God during the many years that she lived her faith on the teeming streets of Calcutta – as evidenced by the letters she left behind – I find it quite human and refreshing. I think it shows that even the most pious and faithfully committed among us is entitled to doubts and misgivings. Far from diminishing her faith and accomplishment, the willingness to question an age-old and tightly defined understanding of God elevates her to an entirely new level of admiration in my eyes. On one hand, she very clearly lived by the principles we all seek in faith – compassion, humility and selfless giving. And on the other, she had the courage to ponder in her own mind, heart and soul the deep mystical questions that surround faith of any kind.

I think back to the "telephone game" we played in class in elementary school. The idea was that the teacher would whisper something to the first kid on the first row of the class and that statement would be sent in hushed voices to the opposite end of the room row-by-row to the last student. What usually came out the other end of the exercise was so completely different from the beginning input that the class would burst out in a grand belly laugh. This is how religion has worked over the past several thousand years – only without the laughter. And the persons we look to for an ultimate insight into life's great eternal questions – our Billy Grahams and our Popes – are really only the next-to-last whisperers in the big classroom of history. While it's not out of the realm of possibility to think that what they have to say is true, and maybe even infallible, it is also perfectly okay to remember that they got the news from somebody else before them. And the folks who kicked it all off thousands of years ago – while they may have had great faith – also thought the earth was flat. It's okay to be skeptical.

So why are we all so quick to accept everything we are told by religious leaders as unquestionable truth? Simply because doing so provides us with an easy way to go – a path with very little or no resistance. It requires no thinking. Even more important, it requires no risk. There is no uncertainty in adopting what has been popularly accepted by the masses throughout the ages. And there certainly *is* risk in wandering off the straight and narrow path to search for something different. Taking the easy path is safe, secure and – of great importance to the vast majority of us – approved by society.

We want to think that our religious idols are learned and wise. They've studied at great religious schools and amassed advanced degrees. They've given themselves elaborate titles and head up large congregations, even entire denominations. They've written books by the score. They measure the lives they've touched in the hundreds of millions. They wear authoritative hats, gowns and robes and sit in fancy chairs on elaborate stages – or wear hip jeans and t-shirts on the stages of today's ultra-cool megachurches.

They have answers – or they seem to – and we like that. They tell us stories that entertain and enlighten us. They use words we may not have heard and impress us with their intellect. They find ways to make even the most arcane statements from scripture tie to something relevant in the confusing world around us. They give us confidence; if we aren't clear on exactly what we should believe, then at least we can believe that they *know* and understand. And that's plenty good for most of us.

But I think we should be justifiably cautious these days about buying into any specific and narrow religious philosophy wholeheartedly – particularly the spiritual vision of a single charismatic individual – without allowing for the proverbial grain of salt. We live in a time when religions have become extremely polarized. Maybe that's due to the power and influence of mass media – television, the Internet, a press that can disseminate information and feelings and opinions around the globe in a matter of seconds. But we seem to feel more strongly and passionately about our own beliefs and less convinced of the rights of others to follow their own. We see other faiths up close and in-person these days, so we're more exposed to the things we might like – or not like – about what they stand for. Or, maybe exposure to other faiths causes us to look more closely at the strange follies and foibles of our own religion; how can we think it odd for another faith to follow such outlandish ideas when we've grown up with a few pretty-darned curious religious customs and traditions of our own?

If I were to fill out a questionnaire that asked for my religious preference, these days I suppose I would check the box marked "Buddhist." I don't really consider myself to be singularly aligned with any specific faith tradition, but I've spent the past several years studying the teachings of the Buddha. The reason I like the Buddhist tradition is because it places far less emphasis on what I believe than it does on how I live my life out in the real world on a daily basis. In fact, after years of casual study, I still have never been presented with a *de facto* list of things that I'm supposed to believe in Buddhism. I have, however, received hundreds of pointers on things I can do every day to live a happier, more fulfilling life out on the freeway. Better still, Buddhism has afforded me an entirely new vantage point from which to view Christianity – the faith of my upbringing – that adds great new perspective, depth and meaning.

All of the monotheistic religions are built around statements of faith that command us to adhere to a very strict doctrine. The Christian Nicene Creed spells out the beliefs of that faith line by line. Evangelicals never say a word without emphasizing belief in submission and the saving power of Jesus. Muslims hinge everything on the statement of faith that *There is but one God and Mohammed is His Prophet* – the Shahada. There's certainly nothing wrong with any of this. It is not my purpose to disprove or disavow any of what the major religions teach – again, I'm not a scholar. But it's been my experience that, while major faiths are pretty heavy-up on teaching beliefs, they sometimes fall a little short on giving us practical tools that will make our lives easier, more peaceful, more serene, indeed more God-like.

In fact, if you take a casual glance at the news on any given day, you can see that the opposite is quite often true. Religions – generally under the control of single-minded leaders – use their beliefs as swords to create division and disharmony between humans and even among nations. The world has become increasingly divided along religious lines – perhaps even more than it always has been along cultural lines. We wield religion as a national weapon now more than ever – even in the United States, where we pride ourselves on plurality, or at least we think we do. America has always been a nation built on faith, but never has it been so overtly Christian in matters of politics and public life as it is today. Right-wingers have done a great job of blurring – or even downright erasing – the line between our national worldview and conservative, evangelical Christianity.

Without proselytizing, I'll say that Buddhism – at least the Westernized version we find here in the United States and in Europe – really avoids the sticky wickets of belief in favor of focusing on compassion, understanding, acceptance and detachment – traits that can help us live much more enlightened lives when put into practice out in the real world on a daily basis. Following the tenets of Buddhism, I can look beyond the rigid dogmas of what a person believes to come to understand that he or she is my kind teacher, perhaps my mother from a previous life, who may be suffering under the delusion that they know the one-and-only correct answer. I can look at conflict through the lenses of poisons like hatred, attachment and ignorance to see that we all operate through false ideas of what is real. By doing this, I can find patience and acceptance in virtually any situation. It's all about love, not hate, isn't it? We have the power to look at anything and everything differently any time we choose to.

Major periods of religious calamity in ages past – notably the Crusades and the Spanish Inquisition – carried hatred and animosity between religions to new heights (perhaps depths would be a better word). But I sense that the polarization that we are currently experiencing in the world has the potential to make these dark chapters in history look like Sunday potluck dinners. In a post-9/11 world, with West meeting East in the major cradles of the Holy Lands, we are staring right into the teeth of what could quickly become the mother of all religious wars. And we should approach that cautiously. As a boy growing up in the United States, I learned in my history classes that we've been engaged in – and won – perhaps twenty major wars. These were all "good wars," and, while I find that phrase somewhat oxymoronic, it still evokes sentiments like freedom, liberty, values, peace and patriotism.

I feel (and fear) that we are currently engaged in the first religious war in our nation's history – even though we don't call it that or choose to view it from that perspective. In fact, we've gone out of our way to not paint the so-called war on terror as a religious war. But others have defined it that way for us. And even though we are basically the undefeated heavyweight champs of the world in our track record for fighting and winning traditional patriotic wars, our record for religious wars has yet to be established. I'm not so sure it's something that we truly comprehend.

My point is this: At a time when religion has taken on an incredible level of importance in political and cultural relations with the rest of the world, we need more than ever to have a realistic, workable idea of what faith and God really are – or what they might mean to others around the world. While it is important – even critical – for us to have an underlying support structure for our societies, a role that religion plays very well, it is equally important for us to not lock ourselves into overly rigid belief systems that give us no leeway, no room to maneuver, no grounds for mutual understanding when we interact with each other. This applies whether we're dealing one-on-one or nation-to-nation. We've got to find ways to back off and agree that we just might all be right.

One of the most interesting parallels I find between Buddhism and Christianity is the belief that suffering in this life somehow leads to greater merit in the next. The central tenet of the Christian tradition holds that Jesus gathered up the sin, pain and suffering of the world into His being and then allowed Himself to be sacrificed on the cross at Golgotha in order that the world He left behind might be saved. Likewise, Buddhism teaches that the greater the suffering one endures in this life, the farther that individual moves toward enlightenment in the next – resulting ultimately, over the course of many incarnations, in achieving a perfect Buddha state. Both faiths, and perhaps other faiths, too, therefore adhere to the notion that those who suffer the most severely in this existence are, in essence, the most godlike.

Having known thousands of individuals in my life thus far, I have come to believe that the world is populated by old souls, young souls, and souls of all ages in-between. And there is no way to tell one from another by outward appearance. I have heard spiritual words of brilliance flow from the mouths of raggedy teenagers, and I have heard hate-filled drivel spew forth from the lips of vaunted spiritual leaders. All of which tells me that we perhaps need to keep a constant critical ear on those whom we allow to speak to us on behalf of God. Does a televangelist or megachurch pastor who earns millions by spreading the good word to the masses really have anything in common with the Jesus who lived out His life among the castaways and downtrodden?

The man behind the dumpster, in my view, shouldered a far greater load than the privileged among us. Perhaps he struggled with mental disease or with alcohol or drug addiction. Perhaps he was once a successful businessman who lost everything through one misfortune or another. Certainly these things happen in the blink of an eye to anyone – they happen every day. Perhaps this man suffered the tragic loss of loved ones, or even an entire family. Perhaps he was chosen to shoulder the burdens of Job from the Old Testament, in which case he would surely be among God's select favorites. Yet we as a society might tend to marginalize him. While we may follow our religious convictions and provide him with food, clothing, our pocket change, a kind word, or even a Bible, would we genuinely pay attention to his spiritual ideas? Is he of less value to us than a Billy Graham or a Pope? Does he know more – or less? And what about the rest of us? Is what we believe of lower value than what we are encouraged to embrace from the often well-heeled mortals whose messages we blindly accept as truth?

I believe that it is perfectly okay to follow some universal source of power that drives our world without getting overly wrapped up in the dogmas of religion. Holy men – some divinely inspired – tell us what they know and what they have studied and learned. We can focus on the goodwill and intent of what they have to say and trust that they are good men and well intentioned – for the most part. But we can also accept religious teachings for exactly what they are – humankind's very best attempt to explain that which cannot be adequately explained – thereby releasing ourselves to open wide our eyes and peer into the bright light of what we do not know. Better yet, we can simply acknowledge comfortably that we know absolutely nothing – which is perfectly fine. And accept that the enormity of truth will be revealed to us only in that first fractional second of death. Only then will we truly understand. And until then, we are fine merely acknowledging that there is some marvelous and mystical promise that exists for us in the Great Beyond.

So let's celebrate our Billy Grahams and our Popes. Let's value them as the very human leaders of institutions that give us structure and meaning. Let's listen to what they have to say – because again, a spiritual truth is a spiritual truth no matter where it comes from. But let's also let them off the hook for being anything other than men who seek truth just like the rest of us. While they may have more of the trappings of religious authority than we do, they must also end up asking the same big questions we will all ask when faced with our own very personal exits from this life. There is no executive wing or penthouse floor in Heaven. We are all equal in God's eyes.

Let's accept that we're all wandering, seeking and searching – some more than others – and that is exactly as it should be. We can help each other, counsel each other, guide each other and love each other. Let's meditate on life and God and pray for true enlightenment. And not forget the less fortunate who may have passed in the night.

Buddhists have a mantra that is said when a life – any life – is ending: *Om Mani Padme Hum.* It is an appeal for the dying creature to reach out and grasp as much suffering as possible to carry away from this difficult world – both as a way to earn merit in the next plane and also to leave a better life behind for others in this one. Just as Jesus did at Calvary.

For the man behind the dumpster:

Om Mani Padme Hum.

Seven: Living Without *Without*

If you go into a restaurant anywhere in the Spanish-speaking world and order *un botilla de agua* – a bottle of water – the first thing the servidor will ask you is *sin gas?* They sell a lot of bottled water in most of the world outside of the United States, and apparently there is a sizeable enough demand for carbonated water – the fizzy kind that tastes sort of like a fountain soft drink without the syrup – that most waiters are obliged to ask whether you want water with or without all the gassy bubbles. *Agua con gas* comes with… and *agua sin gas* comes without.

So, those Latin classes are coming back to you now? You recall that the word *sine* literally translates to *without?* Somewhere along the road to today's understanding of religion, the word sin came to mean a specific thing or set of things or actions instead of a state of being. It came to define something wrong that we do, or a list of all the wrong things we can do, in our lives. A sin is a crime, a misdeed, a mistake, an error in judgment, a wrongful action, a heinous thought – a violation of God's intent for us, in thought, word or deed. In today's society – particularly in our religious world – a sin is something for which we have to answer – in confession, on our knees – in order to receive redemption and salvation.

Or is that what sin means, literally? Instead of a thing, I think the word "sin" – at least in spiritual terms – much more accurately defines a condition. When we are living in sin, we are really living outside the presence of, or farther away from, the connection we absolutely must have with our Creator. And I think that when divinely inspired teachers like Jesus came to the world to share and preach, the real message they brought was all about closing that gap between where our lives typically are, and where they can and should be if we are to feel completely in tune with God. Whatever God is.

Scriptures define Jesus as a great many things: A judge, a doctor, a philosopher, a code enforcement officer (clearing the money changers from the temple), a carpenter, a fisherman, a shepherd and even a military leader. But for the next few paragraphs, I want to present Jesus as a math teacher. Yes, I think all of His worldly messages can be wrapped up in a simple mathematic formula.

$$a + b = c$$

In this equation, a describes where I am today in my normal state of existence. I'm human. I strive. I fail. I seek. I wake each day and marvel at the wonders of the world while also lamenting the horrors and injustices that surround me. I hurt, I rejoice, I thrive and I suffer. Probably pretty much just like you. The product of the equation – c –

describes where I want to ultimately be in this life or the next. Call that Heaven. Or Nirvana. Or Shangri-La. Or Paradise. Or the Pure Land. Or whatever you choose. That's the place I can aim for as I seek, grasp and develop God's will for me in this life that presently surrounds me. The difference between today's current state and that ultimate desired state is, of course, the missing addend b. That is sin. That is the gap between where I am today and the perfect world of my Creator. That is the span of *without* that I must work to fill in order to achieve satisfaction both in this world and in whatever existence may come afterward. In short, that is the sum total of my sin.

Of course, all sacred scriptures carry an immense amount of information on specific things that we should avoid doing if we want to close the gap of without in our lives. The most notable list would be the Ten Commandments. Who could argue that it is wrong to steal, murder, be disrespectful of our parents or want those things that rightfully belong to another man or woman? These actions are certainly things that, if carried out in our lives, will draw us farther and farther away from the oneness we all strive to feel with God. So, in that sense, these types of actions have come to define sin. In popular usage, they have become sins. And there is nothing wrong with looking at these inappropriate actions as "sins," because they definitely serve to increase the value of b and distance us from the perfect state that we desire in our lives.

But somewhere along the winding path of human history, we took this basic idea and – as humans are wont to do – expanded it and elaborated on it and built it into a highly complex moral code. The simple idea of living without without has evolved into very real sets of laws. Indeed, major legal cases continue to bubble up around us involving the display of the Ten Commandments in courthouses and other public venues all across the United States. In the

Islamic world, this moral code has been taken even further, with the *Sharia Law* of the Koran actually providing the foundation for entire societies and legal systems.

In the Episcopal Church, which many only half-jokingly refer to as "Catholic Lite®," the liturgy, customs and beliefs are largely the same as the church of St. Peter with the exception of a belief in and reliance on the Pope as Jesus' man-in-charge here on the terrestrial plane. You may recall from history that King Henry VIII, regent of England, broke that country away from the Roman Catholic Church – and away from the religious control of the Pope – because of the church's refusal to grant him an annulment in his marriage to Catherine of Aragon. Think of that – a major denomination created for want of a simple divorce. But all of this stems from the central fact that the Roman Catholic Church proclaimed then – and still does today – that divorce is a sin. Is it? I don't know, and it's not for me to say.

I, like roughly half of all adults in the Western world, have been through a divorce and feel okay with that. Instead of being something that pulled me farther away from God, I think the quest for personal fulfillment and happiness in this life brings us ever closer to God's presence. To me, failure to fix problems and resolve issues in our lives, especially when they involve making major decisions like choosing whether or not to divorce, is really and definitely something that expands the sin gap. So who knows?

But growing up in the Episcopal Church gave me enough of a glimpse into the uniquely Catholic view of sin to marvel at how human hands throughout history have taken the noble and simple idea of living without closeness to God to elaborate extremes. Indeed, Catholic theologians and policymakers over the ages have created a structure around the notion of sin that's almost comical in its complexity.

For starters, sins come in different levels. As humans, we crave structure – so we've built an elaborate and confusing framework around sin. A quick Internet search on "types of sin" highlights both the complexity and the confusion. One Web site says there are basically only two types of sin – mortal and venial. Another points to three varieties – imputed sin, inherited sin and personal sin. Yet another outlines five types of sin – transgression, unrighteousness, omission of duty, faithlessness and foolish thinking. Still another site points to seven types of sin – the "seven deadly sins" of pride, envy, lust, sloth, gluttony, greed and wrath. All of these sets of sins are set within a matrix of ordinal and cardinal sins – some that can be fixed and others that cannot.

And, of course, to remedy this intricate weave of misdeeds, the church has constructed an equally elaborate system of fixes – starting with confession, but also sometimes involving transgression and ultimately working through justification, purification, sanctification and redemption all the way to salvation. Not to take all of this too lightly – because I do believe that there is absolute good in the quest to bring ourselves always closer to God and reduce the amount of without in our lives – I've always thought that the whole Christian concept of working toward salvation would make a really great board game, sort of like *Monopoly*. We each get a game piece, and we play by rolling the dice (isn't life really like that anyway?) to move forward down the path toward an ultimate destination. Along the way there are a multitude of temptations, errors, slip-ups, challenges and opportunities to develop and grow and learn those things – love, forgiveness, humility – that bring us closer to perfection. *Ooops! I sinned, so three steps back...*

Dante Alighieri took this notion to ultimate extremes in *The Inferno*, outlining in great detail all of the causes and conditions at each of his levels of Hell. His in-depth description of suffering at each plane underscores the incredible complexity surrounding our beliefs in sin and damnation. It was all a divine comedy – or was it?

So how does this new thinking about sin fit into the larger challenge of finding a God that truly works for us in our real-world daily lives? For me, a more realistic understanding of the concept of sin helps to broaden the scope of my moral behavior and enables me to focus more clearly on the bigger goal: being God-conscious and trying to make sure that all of my human efforts point in the general direction of oneness with both the world around me and with my Creator. Of course, I will always strive to uphold the high moral code outlined in works like the Ten Commandments; the universal truths outlined in all the scriptures of all the major religions are as much the product of man's real-world practical common sense as they are divine revelation.

But by clearing away all the dogmas and arcane focus on board-game anti-sin rules and regulations, I can actually conduct my life to a higher standard. I do my best at all times to simply act as I believe my God would have me. As Erma Bombeck so eloquently explained many years ago, we learned nearly all that we need to know to be successful in this life playing in the sandbox in kindergarten. Play well with others. Show proper respect for all people, places and things. Clean up our messes as we make them. Apologize when we have been wrong. Be positive and happy. Try to add more to the world than we take. It's a simple plan for living that works.

Following a personal code like this – developed in direct daily contact with the God of my understanding – leaves me much less wiggle room than simply conforming to the rigid rules and procedures of religion's sin structure, which I find somewhat ironic. It lets me put my head on the pillow each night with a clear conscience. I can go beyond listening to what others might define for me as sins, and follow my own divine guidance – working in close conjunction with the God of my understanding – to believe the things and do the things that truly help to close the gap between where

I am in my life and the perfection that my Creator desires for me. That, to me, is a tougher calling. One that makes faith very real for me.

Of course, there are facets of the popular meaning of sin that are highly valid and fit easily within this broader understanding of God's math. The idea of confession, for one, bears great merit. And all religions have, in one form or another, at least some practice of the ritual of self-revelation. I have found, personally, that when I open up my innermost life to at least one other person, I feel very liberated. The Twelve Steps of recovery as outlined in Alcoholics Anonymous are largely hinged around the fourth and fifth steps, which are, respectively, taking an accurate inventory of one's life and sharing this moral evaluation with another person. I believe that we all harbor secrets – the little nuances that define the darker sides of our inner natures. These are those tiny tidbits that make up the "thoughts, words, and deeds" referred to in Christian liturgy. We all have them, without exception. And I have found that very little that I have shared with anyone in my life, and anything that has likewise been shared with me, has ever raised too much of an eyebrow. In this way, what the televangelists have to say is accurate: we are all, in fact, "sinners."

So if it is true that we are all merely as spiritually ill as the secrets we harbor, then one sure-fire way to make a big dent in that mathematical addend b, is to open up our lives, in a respectful and logical way, to the world around us. It's the ultimate cleansing process. I recall that when I did my first inventory as part of my recovery, I set aside a full weekend. I assembled a notebook and a stack of fresh pens. I found a quiet place to write. And then I proceeded to go completely insane for the next two days. I discovered that those who suggested that I write down an assessment of my moral standing were onto something. For I could not lie to myself as I wrote. I may have been able to convince myself of the lightness of my thoughts and shortcomings in conversations, alone and within the tightly constricted confines of my own head, but I could not do so on paper. And it was this open revelation that became the basis for my healing insanity.

For the first time in my entire life, I took an honest evaluation of myself. I instantly discovered patterns – fears, insecurities, self-doubts, and selfish motivations – that had always been the driving forces behind my life. While I may have had at least some idea of these factors and the roles they had played in my outward actions, I had never up to that point seen them displayed so clearly, so blatantly. Armed with this new knowledge, I was able to see at least the direction I would need to go in order to close the gap that existed in my life at that time between myself and the warm spiritual comfort I so craved.

When the weekend was over, and I was done with my work – emotionally and physically exhausted by the process – I shared it all, word-for-word, with a trusted friend. Not a cleric or counselor but just a friend whom I respected and whom I knew would bear the vital workings of my life with confidence and non-judgment. Once done, I stashed the notebook away at the bottom of a box of old papers and innocuous personal things, hopefully never to be viewed by prying eyes. In my mind, the work had become my Achilles Heel – the epitome of vulnerable weakness that could be used at some point later in my life to bring me down or cause shame and embarrassment. It represented my Holiest of Holies, the bare essence of my faulted life laid bare for a curious world to see.

Years later, as I sorted through old boxes and papers struggling to clean away the flotsam and jetsam that accumulate on their own about my life in preparation for a move to a new home, I ran across the notebook. I opened it to discover a title page very similar to the dire warnings etched into stone at the grand entrance to King Tut's tomb –

curses and ill wishes to whomever invaded these sacred and private papers and an admonishment to leave immediately and forever forget the document's existence. Fumbling through the several-dozen pages, I laughed out loud. Nothing I read meant a thing to me. In fact, not a word there would have likely meant anything to anyone – certainly not the people who now made up the inner circle of my life. Such is the power of sharing our true thoughts, words and deeds with at least one other of God's creatures. Such is the force of opening up to the world. In doing so, we become a part of humankind – no more or less important than any of our fellows – instead of remaining an island unto ourselves.

Something else that I learned as a part of this process – and this is perhaps the most important lesson, at least for me – is that self-revelation is, in fact, a process. One that becomes, with practice and time, a working part of our lives. Knowing my weaknesses and shortcomings – those things that fill the broad gap between a and c – makes them easier to spot as I go through my daily routine. I am not perfect, nor will I ever be. But the process of examining my life within this new context of sin gives me a way to genuinely strive for a higher standard of daily conduct and a true path for moving ever closer to the big gray area that I think of as divinity.

But there is more. What I think must be coupled with the things that I *do*. It's that thing about faith without works, remember? Knowing my shortcomings and having a clear picture of where I have erred in my life give me a fairly clear moral code to follow in my all of my actions moving forward. I have learned that each time I make an apology to someone I may have wronged, for even the simplest thing, I take a solid chunk out of the sin gap.

In the depths of my alcoholism, during the dark two years between my brother's death and my first tenuous steps toward recovery, I did a very wrong deed to one of my closest friends, someone who had stuck by me and remained among the few willing to help me. I acted for selfish reasons and had found ways in my own mind to justify my behavior without having to look honestly at the backlash or hurt feelings I definitely caused. Having no tools – or sense of God – at the time, and not wanting to acknowledge any wrongdoing on my part, I ended the friendship. Doing so presented the path of least resistance to me. Walking away from the mess was easier than stopping to clean it up.

A decade later, listening to bad jokes around the fire at an Indian Guides campout with my son, I heard my friend's name mentioned. The world is always small when it's supposed to be. I was filled almost immediately with one of those hurting aches that wrap around my heart and reach up through my body to poke so annoyingly at my mind. I resolved to reach back across the span of years to do what I needed to do – acknowledge my mistake and make things right. First thing on Monday following the weekend camping trip, I wrote a letter with my very simple apology and best wishes. I made no excuses, and I never used the word "but." I simply owned up to my poor behavior and apologized and dropped the note in the mail. Two weeks later, in a meeting at a client's office, in walked my friend. We shook hands, and then hugged. Not a word was spoken about the letter or what had happened a decade earlier. Nothing was necessary. And we have been good friends for many years since. In fact, I have been blessed by the closeness of a friendship for twenty years – minus ten in the middle – that has survived and thrived.

I aim for the right things, and I take action. Faith does the rest. A God that works in my life fills the gap.

Having written more than my share of employee-training manuals, I know that there are basically two ways to teach people. One way is very linear – take this part and bolt it to the other part and then attach those two parts to a third to make a larger assembly. The other way is to educate the worker to understand how the finished product is supposed to work and how the various components operate together to do whatever it is the widget does. This second method is far more complex, but also far more meaningful, for we are giving someone not only the "what" but also the "why." While humans and religions have done what humans and religions seem to do best – over-thinking, over-reaching and over-organizing the idea of sin to the point where we live our spiritual lives by rote – we, as individuals who are blessed with a direct connection to whatever God created us, have the opportunity to reclaim our own processes for thinking and understanding the real intent and meaning behind the notion of *without*. I believe that we are capable of doing much more than simply following a set of rules. Great spiritual thinkers and teachers – Jesus, Mohammed, the Buddha and many others – have lived in our world to show us the way. They have given us through their lives and teaching the formula for achieving oneness with a God that works.

And I like the way that adds up.

EIGHT: LETTING GO OF LOSS

As I am putting together my thoughts for what to say about loss – likely a prime concern for anyone who's searching for a God that works – I am sitting in the lobby of my veterinarian's office waiting to see the doctor about a favorite pet. Boston-the-Cat, so named because he was found as a kitten – a stray – feeding on scraps outside the dumpster at a Boston Market restaurant, is ill. He has lost a lot of weight over the past two months – about a third of his body mass, as far as I can tell – and I am not anticipating good news. I know that when a kitty loses that kind of weight so suddenly, it usually points to kidney failure. Most all cats eventually succumb to kidney failure or something related. But this great, floppy, always-purring orange tabby is only eight years old, and that seems far too young for such a fate.

I have been through this drill before. I think that when we adopt pets, we already know deep down in our hearts that we will outlive them. We accept that as inevitable, much like the rise and fall of the tides or the arc of the sun and moon across the sky. But that never makes losing them any easier. Pets in our culture are far more than domesticated animals; they become like children, members of the family. I read a marketing study once for an advertising client that said pet owners are willing to spend as much for pets as for their children in many cases. Selling everything from high-grade foods to advanced pet health care – even surgery – is a multi-billion dollar industry.

When we, as humans and loving partners, sit on the cusp of hearing bad news about any of our loved ones – pets and family members or friends alike – we begin to prepare ourselves internally for the loss that we know is about to come. We gird ourselves for an empty spot and the shake-up that is sure to occur in our lives. I recall that when I lost my brother so suddenly back in 1988, I confronted the unexpected realization that the fabric of my original family – a father, mother, older sister, younger brother and myself – had quite suddenly been ripped apart and tossed away. A circle originally made up of five arcs had to reform itself with four, and each part had to learn to deal with a new sense of relationship to the rest. I had always been a middle child – and had always given myself that unique context in life. Yet now I was the youngest of my nuclear family, and that brings with it an altogether different feeling. When we face loss, we are forced by events beyond our control to reassess ourselves and the roles we play in the stark new world that has been thrust upon us.

And so I dig out my game face – the one I have used when going through many various forms of loss over the years – and dust it off and prepare to don it again. And a part of my heart prepares itself for the knot that I know will come – and the empty spot I will eventually find at the foot of my bed. In a way, I can sense it there already.

There are a great many things that those around us have to say when we experience a loss – all well meaning. These are bromides that, it is hoped, will help us to quickly and easily set the loss aside and move forward with our lives, even though it is known by all that the loss of any significant part of our world – even a household pet – is never dealt with quickly or easily. These things that people say – words of condolence that often trivialize unexplained or sudden loss with sentiments that neither giver nor receiver actually believe – are well-intended ways of perhaps moving us speedily through the stages of grief to land sooner at the final place of acceptance. At the very least, they give us nice things to say when we having nothing better to offer.

And so we accept these heartfelt assurances from the well-intentioned persons who know us – even arcane sentiments like *God needed a new statue for His garden* – and stuff them away and turn inward to deal with the pain we feel in the best way we can, using whatever tools we have. Sometimes that means simply stumbling through it – placing one foot in front of the other – until we walk back out into the sunlight again. There simply is no process yet developed by man that creates any shortcuts for going through the clearly defined stages of grief. While we may delay a step or two – packing anger away to eat at our hearts, causing us to question God, or even denying that we may be in denial – we are forced to deal with all of them eventually, completely and in our own way.

The bulk of the nominally helpful bits of insight and wisdom I have received from others when I've experienced loss, or have heard shared back and forth between others I know at life's grieving times, all tie back to God in some way. Knowing not what else to say, or having no clue how to make sense of a tragic loss, we invoke a *Not Me* mentality and point to God as the mastermind behind all plans. It's easy to say that God is the source of our loss and, in the same breath, say that God caused the loss to happen for some reason that is for our unknown and unexplained ultimate benefit. Which leaves us perplexed at best – and confused or angry at worst.

I could not have seen it coming, but I fell into a deep state of depression during the two years following by brother's sudden death. I look back at those two years – marked at one end by a week's worth of surrealism, a funeral and the feeling that the entire event was some sort of bad dream lived out on an otherworldly stage, and my stumbling arrival at the doors of recovery on the other – as the darkest period of my life. I do not recall seeing colors; the world seemed drab and gray in a very real sense. Every day was a test of endurance, which increasingly ended with me drinking or drugging myself into oblivion. On more than one occasion, I found myself alone and isolated, holding a phone in one hand and a loaded gun – *I really hate guns* – in the other and not knowing which to use; one solution I knew would bring relief, and the other, I was confident, would bring sweet release. But always, the thought that my death would be measured by the yardstick of my brother's heroic fall – accompanied by full military honors, jet fly-bys and the presentation of folded flags and medals – was powerful enough to pull me back away from the abyss. I also had an infant daughter, several months old, who, as much as anything gave me enough of the breath of life to keep going for another day.

As part of this deep, deep depression, I became obsessed with the concept of death. I had never truly experienced death; my only previous contacts had been the passing away of elderly aunts, uncles, a grandparent or two – the types of passing on from this world that we take for granted as children growing up. Each of these events seemed as much an opportunity to catch up with relatives as anything else. But death now stalked me. I was overwhelmed with the thought that death could and would occur at any time – to you, the neighbors, my coworkers, all of the people who surrounded me. I became obsessed with every story of death I heard or read in the news. Airplanes seemed to crash daily. I reached a point where I would not drive on a freeway, fearing that a deadly accident lurked with every lane change. And then I learned that accidents happened more frequently at neighborhood intersections. I became, in a very real way, paralyzed by life, venturing out to the grocery store only when absolutely necessary and, then, only in the middle of the night when I knew it would be inhabited solely by stock boys pushing dollies of cardboard boxes, and other vampires like me. I withdrew from the world of the living and hid out in my own dark zone of solitude.

I say all of this only to point out that, despite the very best of intentions of everyone in my circle of friends, family and acquaintances at that very fragile and vulnerable period of my life, none of the pat answers that were meant to help me deal with the confusion of loss had any positive impact whatsoever. Nothing worked, certainly not bland attributions that pointed to God.

What did help – tremendously – was an all-new understanding, developed slowly over time and through great pain, of how I should deal with loss in my life. What I ultimately discovered was simple: *there really is no such thing as loss.* Loss implies that once something is gone, then a negative space remains behind, and the world is somehow lessened or made smaller by what is missing. And that is simply not the case. The First Law of Thermodynamics states that energy can be neither created nor destroyed. It may change states or forms – motion produces friction, which changes to heat, which converts water into steam, which drives an engine, which creates – of course – motion. And the items that surround us – the people, the things, the jobs and even the pets – are like that, too. When something disappears, it is not gone entirely; we are still left with memories if nothing else. And our lives are in some way enriched by the experience of having enjoyed whatever it was that we believe has been lost.

So, in this sense, loss is a false concept. The Bible says that from dust we come and to dust we will all eventually return. I know that the molecules that make up my body – hydrogen, nitrogen, carbon, oxygen and a host of other chemicals and compounds – were likely a part of some living thing that existed in the millions of years that passed before my time. And, as the world hopefully continues to spin in the years following my death, I trust that those same molecules will become a small part of some other organism – plant or animal life – and on and on through the marvelous cycles of nature. I have always been amazed by the beautiful and poetic structure of the natural world – the way that leaves falling to the ground each Autumn break down into nutrients that, in turn, fertilize the generations of trees to come. There is a brilliant ongoing pattern to our world – and loss is simply one point on the cycle. And all points are symbiotic, too; without birth there is no death, and without an end there can be no new beginning.

Along with this goes the idea – and this has really been the key to me – that *I own nothing in this world.* My brother was not mine to own, any more than he belonged to my mother or father or to the United States Marine Corps. He was a part of this world and belonged solely to it – and to the force that created everything. For me to mourn for something that I never owned is to be immensely selfish – like feeling sorry for losing something that was never mine. Instead, I look at the inevitable losses around me as mere transitions – gifts in my life changing form from something I have known or even loved to a memory that now becomes part of the rich mosaic of my life. Surely I miss my brother, as much as I know that I will miss my treasured pet, but these are not my things to miss. They have been gifts given to me in my life by the world – *by God, if you will* – to enjoy one day at a time. When they are gone, I simply must be thankful that they have blessed and enriched me. And I know that something equally wonderful will take the place of each thing that is gone – just like the constantly changing state of energy.

Native Americans have long known this, which is one of the reasons why European settlers were able to take advantage of them so easily through treaties. Many Indian tribes had no concept of ownership in the form commonly understood by early colonists and settlers. To them, each person and each animal – even the trees in the forest that were chopped down to create shelter and cooking fires – were all part of something much greater and grander than any single person or thing. Everything was to be shared by all. And when hunters went into the field to claim a deer or elk for food, their first act was to give thanks to the animal for offering itself up for the benefit of the other living beings with which it shared a common world.

An amazing photographic article appeared some years ago in one of my favorite magazines, *National Geographic.* It was a visual essay that captured a subject rarely seen by humans – the pursuit of a moose by a wolf in the wild. Through masterful tracking and clever camouflage, the photographer was able to follow the lengthy hunt between a healthy, voracious and dominant predator and its older, weaker prey. After repeated attacks, each repelled at the cost of some damage to the latter, the former – in keeping with nature's undeniable way – finally prevailed. I found the story brutal, bloody and disturbing in a way – captured vividly by a world-class photographer – but also beautiful and majestic. There came a distinct moment near the end of the day-long hunt, when the moose ceased its flight and turned to face its attacker. There was an unspoken exchange between the two, a show of mutual respect, and an open acknowledgment that each was fulfilling its role in the intricate machinery of the natural world. Finally, with a bow of its head, the moose dropped down on its front knees and surrendered itself to a worthy and rightful partner in life. From the dust of the world we all come, and to the dust of the world we must all eventually return.

And so I see the passing of people and places and times and things as a rhythmic part of the beauty and organization of God's world. And I am awe-struck and humbled by the elegant simplicity of it all. I try to look at every passing thing in my life as a gift.

But it is normal, I think, for us humans to fear death. We naturally avoid that which we do not know or understand. It is surely a great benefit for armies that soldiers entering the service are mostly eighteen or nineteen year-olds – just boys and girls, really. They feel invulnerable and, quite literally, bulletproof. *The "world of hurt" will always happen to someone else.* We fear death because we have no real idea of what comes next. So we hang on fervently to the life that we know, even when it is obvious that life, as we know it, might have long ago left on its own. Medical ethicists routinely deal with this quandary; there is a difference between what we *can* do to save a life, and what we *should* do. A good veterinarian will explain it this way: we make the decision to end the life of a pet based on what is best for *them,* not what we think is best for *us.*

Boston-the-Cat has not been my first. Ten years ago, I stood in a darkened room – a vet's office – looking at x-rays of Pepper-the-Dog, my mottled blue merle Australian Shepherd. She had been with me for many years and had helped to teach both of my children to walk – at the cost of significant discomfort to herself – by offering them the grip of the lovely long hair that graced her hind legs. Two weeks earlier, she had missed an appointment – failing to show up at my feet beneath my desk as I rose to work early. I found her on the floor in the hallway, breathing heavily. I rubbed her behind the ears and made a note to keep an eye on her throughout the day.

Now, on a light box mounted on the vet's wall, I saw an image of Pepper's body that looked strangely like a gumball machine. She was filled with what looked to me like tiny water balloons. The cancers had come out of nowhere and grown prodigiously to rob my precious companion of breath or even the energy to pick herself up to move. Yet I still saw the love, the desire to come to me, the eagerness to lick my children's faces as they arrived home from school and be a part of our world in her brownish-blue eyes. As expected, the doctor offered me the option that I knew was coming. I made the empty gesture of discussing it with my wife, but there really was no decision to make. It had already been made.

I cradled her in my arms, staring into her unblinking eyes, and did my best to accommodate her labored breathing. She seemed heavy. We did not break our gaze; I wanted to show her a happy, strong and loving face – a false front. I think she knew what was coming. And I think she was grateful. For, however we treat animals or think of their lesser reasoning as inferior intelligence, perhaps they – like the wolf and moose – are infinitely more in-touch with the realities of our natural world than we are.

As the injection took hold and began its errand of mercy, her breathing became gentler, less strained and easier. Until the last heaving motions built to a final gasp and life left her body. Her eyes remained open, staring deeply into mine. I had never up to that time in my life felt such a powerful sense of peace. It overwhelmed me. She seemed much lighter, easier to hold. Pepper gave the most amazing and personal gift – a giver to the end – even though I thought I was the benevolent one. She taught me that I must never fear death. I would draw upon this lesson in the coming years when I was able to hold my mother's hand and offer her strength and love and best wishes for the voyage ahead, even as she had already begun the transition from this world into the next.

While the death of my brother may have been the one calamitous event that caused me to squarely address the questions of faith that had always overshadowed my life, my mother was the catalyst that challenged me and guided me onto the path to spiritual discovery. She served as the classic literary foil – the force that compels change and drives a plot to twist, turn and find its own strange and unpredictable destination. Through that process, we explored the idea of death – indeed, of loss – together. In the end, I was privileged to be with her as she wrote the closing pages of her own final chapter. And, having gained a new concept of the passing from the human world to the spirit world, I handled her death far differently than I had dealt with my brother's – with what I hope was compassion, understanding and acceptance. In the final two days of my mother's life, she completely withdrew from this world, preparing, I believe, for her transition into the next. During that time, I like to think she held the hand of one son in this realm and the hand of another in whatever exists beyond the Great Divide.

And so today I see loss as an opportunity, a chance to try to draw meaning from events in life that often make no sense at all. I will continue to listen politely as others offer well-intentioned sentiments and condolences, even those that point an incomprehensible finger at God. But then I will begin to look for the blessings and lessons I have received and be hugely grateful.

Death is not the end. It is simply a transition – that comes bearing gifts.

We nursed Boston-the-Cat until both children were home from their respective schools for the summer, doing what little we could to offset his failing health and continued weight loss through daily subcutaneous fluid injections. We viewed each chance to pamper him as an opportunity to give thanks for the years of unconditional love he had so freely given. In the end, when we knew the time had come, we were all together with him as a family to accept and share his final gift of peace.

NINE: WHAT OLD PEOPLE KNOW

    For more than thirty years, I have made the occasional drive down to the small village on the Texas coast that I think of as my hometown. I never actually lived there – my parents bought a beach home in that sleepy seaside town in the mid-1970s when they both worked in the oil and gas industry in Houston. I made weekend trips there in those days – on top of an occasional skip day when the beckoning call of zipping across the bay on my sleek little Seahorse loomed larger on my list of things to do than sitting in a windowless classroom out in the bland city suburbs. After high school, I moved off to college and somehow ended up, many moves and several decades later, at my current place of residence some three hundred miles to the north. But distance has never stopped me from hopping in the car, rolling down the windows, finding some really off-beat radio program –

AM stations in rural areas can be great fun – and making the six-hour drive.

After a hundred or more drives like this, I can tell when I'm nearing the home where my father still lives as much by smell as by roadside signs or mileage markers. The air bears the unmistakable scent of the ocean – with a dampness and salty tang that fills the air as the fresh coastal breezes push gently through the shrimp nets that hang to dry on tall poles at the northern edge of town. We all know of a place like this or, if we don't, we should. It's quiet, and peaceful – a world of pastel-colored clapboard houses and barnacle-encrusted pilings. A quick glance through the police blotter of the local weekly paper might mention a minor burglary or two – maybe a shrimp net or a few tools stolen off one of the hundreds of blue-water shrimp boats that call the little village home port. Or a public intoxication or two – perhaps a shrimp boat deckhand unwinding after long weeks at sea. Or an angry captain who lost a shrimp net and some tools.

For the most part, it's a sleepy town anchored at one end by a shallow, scenic bay that stretches across to a long peninsula that makes up a large segment of the barrier islands that run along the Texas coast, and on the other end by the dilapidated and rattlesnake-infested concrete buildings that remain from a World War II-era military airfield that trained B-26 and P-51 pilots. The town hosts little tourism – it has yet to be discovered by the vacationing and beach-home-bound masses from nearby cities who have made all points around Galveston Bay to the north a mass of wall-to-wall condominiums and trendy bungalows. Instead, there are shrimp boats – lots and lots of them – and sagging piers and pebble-strewn beaches where the murky Texas coastal water bleeds gently off toward the deep blue sea that lies outside the bay and beyond the peninsula.

When I pull into town, I drive past a handful of rusty metal buildings that have served over the decades as welding or repair shops for the shrimp boat fleet. And then I pass a wooden shack perched atop a foundation of creosote poles – a restaurant this year. Then I pass a small convenience store that sells little more than fishing licenses, beer, ice and bait. And finally I turn off the main road and onto the drive that winds along the shore of the East Bay and on toward a bend called Grassy Point. My family home is a short walk down from the point, marked in front by an oyster shell driveway and surrounded on all sides by banana and palm trees that sway gently in the steady bay breezes. By far, the home's most prominent feature is a balcony that opens out from the back to perch like a ship's bridge high up above the tall reeds that run like thick, green carpeting out to the muddy water a hundred yards away.

No matter where I am or where I go in my life, I can close my eyes and transport myself to the tranquil setting of that balcony, breathing in the air and taking in a dozen familiar images – a brown pelican perched atop a faded sign that marks the entrance to the brackish channel that runs up to the back yard, a rusting crab trap pulled up on the shore, seagulls drifting lazily over the piles of discarded oyster shells that peek above the water at low tide. These visions are a part of me, as much the building blocks of my make-up as my gender or size or shape. And each time I visit the house, I find my way first to the door that leads out onto the balcony to check to see that the setting remains unchanged – an anchor of sorts on which to ground my ever-changing life. I need to see that the things that are supposed to remain constant in my world do exactly that.

But there is another image that quickly comes to mind when I take the time to close my eyes and picture my town – the image of an elderly man, sitting in the shade on a porch at the side of a home just down the street that looks out to the glittering bay beyond. No matter what time of day I have rolled into town, and even in the chilliest of months, I have looked instinctively to the right immediately after making the turn off the main road onto the lane that meanders down to Grassy Point, and seen the man sitting quietly in a great wooden chair, surrounded by potted plants and other various objects of flotsam that have washed up on his porch over time – a garden rake, a fishing rod, an ice chest, a casting net. I do not recall the first time that I noticed the man, nor do I recall the last. But I know that I have seen him many dozens of times. And generally the image is the same. A quiet man sitting calmly, surrounded by a hodge-podge of simple possessions, staring out toward the ocean, deeply contented.

Years ago, when I was riding high on the crest of my youth, I tended to dismiss the old man – or anything that stood still – as ancillary, extra, stagnant and completely peripheral to my life. My world moved with the speed and excitement of neon. I operated much as I see young people doing today – whirling like a dervish spinning for the sake of spinning and wasting incredible amounts of energy while getting nowhere in the process. That is the gift and the blessing of youth; to possess adrenalin in abundance and drive aplenty while scoffing at concepts like patience or tameness or solitude – or the simple pleasures of sitting on a shaded porch at the edge of the ocean's bountiful wonders to stare at a seagull drifting effortlessly on the wind's invisible currents. For me in those days, time spent idly breathing in the intoxicating scent of a gentle breeze that brings a fresh tale from its ocean visit seemed a waste of time – a roadblock to the excitement and enthusiasm of a fast-paced life, and an obstacle to achieving the goals that I had set out so aggressively for myself.

I have observed that there are generally two types of elderly people in our society today: those who are generously happy and those who aren't. Old people tend to migrate to one extreme or the other – they are unabashedly ebullient, pleasant and fun to be with, or they are bitter, cantankerous, mean and spiteful. There are no absolutes in life; surely there are many people in the golden years who find space in the huge span between these two polar positions. And, of course, living only at the ends of the happy scale isn't limited simply to old people. But if you stop to consider the seniors who inhabit your world, you may tend to agree with my bold assertion. *Old people generally thrive on life in the golden years, or they brood quietly as if waiting for the end.*

I theorize that the major contributing factor to whether we lean toward happiness or bitterness as we pass through the decades of our lives is the ability we get, through maturity, to sit back on our figurative porches and learn to watch the world go by. We either gather up a sense of peace and tranquility and accept that the world we occupy is on balance a good and decent place, or we allow ourselves to be battered and bashed by the struggles of endless troubles and wind up calloused and jaded and less likely to meet the world and its occupants on friendly, open and amicable terms.

One of the really neat things that comes with the opportunity to completely rethink religion at middle age – or to be forced by pains and hurts to wipe the slate clean and develop a new understanding of what all the words and rituals really mean – is the ability to view the things we have heard and seen for years through all-new lenses. In his moving memoir *A Monk Swimming,* Malachy McCourt says that the title of the book came from words said over and over again from earliest youth: *Hail Mary, full of grace, the Lord is with Thee. Blessed art thou a monk swimming.* We all have our own versions of a monk swimming. We have them because we've said prayers – and assumed beliefs – from a time when we were not yet capable of truly understanding them. Over and over again. And, until we stand back and reexamine these meaningless nuggets that we continue to use every day, we will miss the chance to crumple up and toss away the old script that we've been following and start afresh to truly understand what these things can mean to us in our lives and in our quest for a God that works.

For me, one old idea that sat unrecognized before my very eyes for so many years is the phrase from Psalms 46:10 in the Bible, which says quite simply, *Be still and know that I am God.* Like many, I had heard and voiced this phrase over and over again countless times sitting in the pews on Sunday mornings. But I never really knew, or never took the time to stand back and truly think about the importance of these eloquent few words – until forced by crisis in adulthood to learn for myself the genuine spiritual beauty of stillness.

My natural inclination – brought about either by nurture or nature, or by both – is to flit constantly from thing to thing in my life – work, family, hobbies, political issues, the news, events in my community, favorite sports teams, the list goes on. These are not inherently bad things and, in fact, can be generally good things. They add substance to my life. But I find that they can also be inadvertent substitutes for pausing to relax and reflect on who I am and why I am here – I mean *really* – and how I can best snuggle up seamlessly with the idea of what God really is and what I should be doing every day to fully develop my role with my Creator.

I opened a box of Cracker Jacks once as a child and – as is common practice for kids even today – rummaged straight to the bottom to ferret out the prize. The treasure in this instance was one of those flat plastic boxes with the tiny silver BB and lots of small indentations scattered about. The object of the game was to gently shake and lean and tilt the tiny plastic tray until the little ball fell snuggly into one of the dips and came to a halt – still, unmoving, at rest.

I find that all too often in my adult life I am like that little ball, rolling hither and yon, filling up my life with things and activities that I think will fill the empty spaces and lead to some marvelous peace that brings lasting joy and fulfilling answers to my life. If I only meditate hard enough, then perhaps I can achieve Nirvana. If I volunteer to do more, then perhaps I will find the true blissful feelings of serenity that I crave. If I keep shaking and scratching and digging at the same old idea of who or what God is, *then maybe it will be revealed to me in a new, more powerful and meaningful way.*

But what the old man on the porch taught me – what he demonstrated to me by example through all those years – is that if I stop, and breathe, and sit, and simply pause to watch the ceaseless waves of the world roll gently toward me at the shoreline of my life, then I have a far greater chance of finding true peace and serenity. If I stop rolling around endlessly hoping to land in a permanent groove of tranquility, then God will come to me. For the most part, my only job is to be still – and to simply know that there is some controlling power at work in my life.

My two children have grown up in an instant age – the era of the Internet, instant messaging, Twitter, Facebook and cell phones. To them, the prospect of waiting an hour for a response to a text message to a friend – usually just a letter or two, like "k" – is unthinkable. Their world – and increasingly, my world, too – revolves at warp speed. Which means we do more, and do it much faster, than we ever did before. All of which can be a great thing if kept in perspective and managed well. But this frantic pace that we've established for ourselves in daily life can also render as all but impossible our sometimes-desperate attempts to slow down and find the daily peace that is so essential to maintaining a fit spiritual state. The tools of our age may be instant, but our connection to our Creator cannot be. The idea of God is timeless, and so maybe we need to occasionally forget time and still ourselves in order to find its true depth and meaning.

Of course, none of this means that we simply do nothing and never take action; I believe that God always meets me halfway, which implies some movement on my part. The flotsam that washed up on the old man's porch shows the necessary activities of life – a fishing rod points to a walk down to the shore and the quest for daily sustenance, and a garden rake would prove that even the quietest of lives must be accompanied by some labors. But it also means that we can be more selective in our activities, or at least more aware of the countless turns our spinning top takes as we wobble aimlessly across the tabletop of daily life.

As a self-employed writer, I find it difficult to accept the occasional day that's not driven by endless deadlines as the world's little reminder that I'm supposed to relax and take a deep breath every once in a while. Like many, it's logical and natural for me to measure my self-worth and importance in life by how much I am able to accomplish. And, more pragmatically, to not work also means to not eat. I find myself thinking this way, even though I've never in my life gone a day without food or shelter and, in fact, have been blessed with a healthy share of life's simple rewards.

I can count on one hand the number of times in my sixteen-year solo career that I have not had a fairly healthy queue of projects lined up. I gave up wondering if I would be able to eke out a living or not after the first few months – more on that in a later chapter. But I very clearly recall one period a few years ago when one day without work turned into two and then three and then an entire week of sitting idly at my desk. I began to get jittery and nervous, and to squirm and become restless and irritable. Insecurity lives just beneath the surface for most of us. It surely does for me. Finally, I picked up the phone and ran down my list of clients hoping to stir up some activity or shake a project loose. But nothing came – the phone simply would not ring.

One day, after nearly two weeks, the phone did ring, and I found myself speaking to someone in need of my services – a referral from one of my best clients. The woman introduced herself as the executive director of a local not-for-profit group that was looking for help with a brochure. I had come highly recommended, she said – a tribute to my valued client. But she also made it plainly clear that she had no budget whatsoever. This work, if I would agree to accept it, would be *pro bono* – earning me not one thin dime of the income I so badly believed I needed.

Because the referral had come from a client and friend, I felt obligated to do the work – and I had plenty of time on my hands anyway. And so I began to discuss arrangements with her to meet and gather the input I would need to begin writing. As I started to give her details of my office location – this was a freebie, so she would certainly have to come to me – she stopped me abruptly. "Oh, no, you definitely need to come down here," she said. "You really need to see what we're doing before you can write about us."

"I've done lots of brochures like this before," my ego announced to both of us. "So if you'll simply come up or send over some information, then I can…"

"I really think you need to come down to see what we do," she said. "Can you please set aside some time?"

I paused. An inner voice said that I needed to be in my office, squirming at my desk and waiting for the phone to ring with a real project. But I thought of what the client who referred me might think if I made this difficult – selfish thinking, I know. And I agreed to meet her the following morning.

The meeting took place deep in the heart of one of the poorer areas of my city. And within moments of opening the door, I knew why she, in spite of her very demure and quiet nature, had insisted on my driving down to meet her. This organization was doing incredible things to help many who were not in a position to help themselves. I witnessed pure giving – complete selflessness in action. And I felt very humbled and embarrassed and even ashamed of my hesitancy the day before. What started out to be an hour-long input session turned into a full day of learning and seeing with my own eyes the ways that I believe God wants us to give of ourselves. And what started out to be a single payless project evolved into an offer to join the board of directors of this wonderful group, which has grown to become one of the largest and most respected charitable organizations in the city.

My willingness to help, in spite of my focus on selfish needs and the damage my pride and ego might cause, got me out of my self-induced and inwardly focused inertia and quickly into the mode of using my meager skills for the benefit of others. It was a tremendous lesson in humility for me, and it has made a lasting difference in how I operate professionally. I never dismiss out-of-hand a project prior to investigation. In essence, *I had been forced to be still so that the Supreme Being could reveal some greater purpose in my life.*

Interestingly, the day I set myself to work writing the woman's free brochure, my office phone began to ring. And I received over the course of the next few days enough work to easily compensate for the two weeks spent sitting idly. And it has rarely stopped ringing since.

And so I have come to believe that being still and knowing that God will be revealed to me often means little more than doing the simple things that lie in front of me. Instead of wasting energy in my fruitless efforts to create what I think is God's plan for my life, I need only to relax, breathe deeply and wait for quiet messages to give me direction. Like an old man who sits serenely on a porch by the ocean day after day, I can learn to take each moment as it comes, and focus on the tasks that come my way. I can be still and silent, *and know.*

I never met the old man, although I wish now that I had stopped on one of my countless drives by the sagging screens of his quiet porch to say hello and introduce myself. In a small town – especially a quiet village by a peaceful sea

– it is possible to do such a thing. I do not know who he was or where he came from or what led him through the decades of his life to the fading paint of his tilting porch, in the shade of a rustling oak at a simple home on a quiet street next to a tranquil bay. But I want to think that our conversation would have been light and easy and pleasant. We may have discussed the pattern of the tides, the cars that passed by on the street, the neighbor's cat, what the fish were biting. Or quite simply nothing at all. But I missed my chance.

Perhaps it's one of life's greatest ironies that old people – at least the happy ones – have lived long enough to know all the little secrets to living a life that's in synergy with God. I occasionally joke that by the time my children are fully grown, I will know everything I need to know to be a good parent. Wisdom and maturity are like that, too. By the time we get them, we are nearing the end of our opportunity to use them. But the man on the porch, who I sadly have not seen for the past several years as I've made the occasional pilgrimage home, showed me that stillness does not mean lack of purpose any more than drive and activity mean progress or accomplishment.

Maybe if I am still – making myself open to guidance from a source of power far greater than anything I could ever imagine – and work to make sure that the few things I do can be of benefit to others, then I will be blessed with my own gift of a quiet porch on which to sit when I am old.

Ten: Big Church, Little Church

One day several months before my mother passed away, we spent a quiet afternoon together in her hospital room. It was sunny and beautiful outside and I had made the five-hour drive down to see her that morning. She was rested and feeling well and our conversation was gentle and easy. She wanted to know about my wife and me and the kids – *were they enjoying the summer and were they excited to be going back to school, and how was business?* Working for myself affords me a great deal of flexibility and I was making this trip as often as I could, both to check up on her slowly fading physical condition and also to visit with my father and do what I could to support him in his continual care for her.

We covered the pleasantries of my life and then got around to hers. She was always the ultimate optimist – *Oh,*

I have every intention of seeing my grandchildren grow up, she would say. *God wouldn't let me miss that.* And I think that was good for her – attitude is ninety percent of everything in life. I know that patients who have strong faith and believe that they will improve often do. But the reports from the doctors and the diminishing results from her many treatments had begun to tarnish our enthusiasm. Her cancer had spread slowly at first, beginning in her breasts, but then migrating over the course of two years to envelope her bones and then her lymph nodes. She now had a large tumor inside her head that was placing great pressure on her eyes and causing significant headaches. Constant double vision had forced the doctors to stitch her left eye closed permanently, and so she looked out at the world with one eye only.

She had been a trooper from the beginning, making one change and then another in her lifestyle and undergoing a continual regimen of chemotherapies and radiation treatments over the course of many months with varying degrees of success. My father had been her constant companion through it all – spending days, weeks and months by her side during countless visits to the major medical centers in Houston, and now here to the regional hospital in Victoria, a scant sixty miles from home. But despite her ever-positive outlook for the future, it was slowly dawning on all of us that, though she might win a minor skirmish here or there, the outcome of her battle was largely decided.

As she gave me a rundown on the most recent updates from one doctor or another – and when she expected to once again be able to sleep in her own bed at home, and which medications made her feel better and which didn't – I noticed her glancing more and more up toward the television monitor that hung in the corner of the room above the chair in which I sat. The volume had been down since I had arrived, so I hadn't even noticed that the set was on. We continued our conversation – flitting as we normally did from topic to topic – but I sensed her slowly being drawn to whatever program was playing on the tube overhead. It was mid-afternoon, so I naturally assumed it to be a soap opera, the matinee flick, or – more likely – a re-run from a favorite old sit-com.

"Let me guess – *Green Acres*," I offered with a smile, pointing upward. The show had long been one of her favorites and she had made it a goal to collect nearly every episode on tape so that she could view them again over and over. There had been a time several years earlier when she would call me in the middle of the day to tell me about an episode she had just watched, sharing in great laughing detail the antics of Oliver and Lisa and Eb and Mr. Drucker and Mr. Haney and Hank Kimball. She loved the show, and I did, too, and we would laugh and say *remember when they all got together and...* and then we would end each call with I love you and I would return to my work smiling, happy and thankful. But Arnold, the Ziffel's clever pig, or the other zany denizens of Hooterville, were not the fare on her TV this day.

"No," she said. "I haven't been watching much of that lately." I was curious. So I got up out of my seat and walked over to her side by the bed to see for myself what could possibly be the cause of such distraction.

On the screen a preacher in a tailored pinstriped suit with shiny French cuff links strode forcefully from one end of a large flower-laden curved stage to the other, arms lifted high in the air, waving a Bible, and exhorting his followers to absorb the full meaning of some particular verse of scripture. He stopped occasionally and, with eyes squinting and face beet-red, held the Bible aloft and waved it and stabbed at it with the other hand and then pointed out to the crowd and made some exclamatory statement. The camera shot would switch to a wide-angle pan of the crowd all lifting their arms and crying and shouting amen. A Bible verse would scroll across the bottom of the screen and a phone number would blink in bold type.

"Nope, that's not *Green Acres*," I said. "Definitely not Green Acres."

She chuckled. "No, definitely not," she said. "But I do find myself watching it more and more."

I was surprised. Not that she was tuning into religious broadcasting – that seemed to me to be one of those deeply logical things a sick person might do in a hospital. But it was the nature of the programming that gave my eyebrows cause to rise. My mother was a deeply devout and religious person – and had been all her life. From my earliest years, I had seen in her a complete and total devotion to faith and God. But her spiritual allegiance had been to the quiet and ceremonious Episcopal Church – never to fire-breathing Pentecostal televangelists. Her attraction to this now struck me as odd, and I thought back almost instantly to the living room antics of my younger brother, whose comic stock-in-trade had always been the over-animated big-haired TV preacher. *Send me your munnnaaay tooodayyah!* he would say, drawing each word out to four full syllables. *VISA, MasterCard, American Express...*

We had playfully mocked the pompadour-coiffed TV preachers – all of us – for as long as I could remember. We saw them as different, linked up with some other brand of God, purveyors of a fast-food kind of religion that was nothing at all like the pious and candle-lit ritual world of Father Martin with his chiming bell. We had seen them as the comic relief of religion, stereotypical caricatures of themselves who pulled chicken livers out of peoples' heads before pushing them backwards into the waiting arms of assistants at big-tent revivals.

"Hey, whatever floats your boat," I said. "Has he asked you to send in your *munnnaaay tooodayyah* yet?" She giggled. But then she said something that caught me completely by surprise. She spoke in a measured and confiding tone, as if revealing a deeply hidden secret.

"You know, I'm starting to think that if I had it to do all over again I would have headed down this route," she said, nodding to the preacher on the screen. "These guys get straight to the point and tell it like it is – everything, right out of the Bible – they really focus on the *Word*."

I thought back to a Sunday morning in my very early youth – maybe around the age of seven or eight – when I was allowed to skip the customary children's Sunday school and join my parents in the adult service. We sat in a pew near the front of the church. I had just celebrated a birthday, and I think it was customary to allow children celebrating some special occasion to accompany their parents to the altar rail during Holy Communion for a blessing. When the time came for the congregants to stand and file row-by-row up to the altar rail to receive the bread and wine, she leaned over and whispered sternly into my ear to keep my head bowed and my arms by my side. Head down, hands folded together, arms down by your side. Got that? I nodded.

Of course, in my mind I was already wondering how I was supposed to get my hands up to receive the thin wafer of bread with my arms nailed to my side. I did not know that I was only to receive a priestly hand on the head and a birthday blessing – it would be several more years before I would undergo confirmation, thereby earning the right to receive Holy Communion. And so when I somehow managed to pull off the contortion of lifting my folded hands upward to the rail with my head bowed and arms fixed to my side, my mother reached over with an astonished look and firmly pushed them down again. Once back in the pews, her furrowed brow left little doubt that I had stepped far outside the boundaries of proper religious etiquette, violating the solemnity of a highly revered sacramental moment. I am confident that I spent the rest of that day wondering if my blessing had been penalized accordingly.

To her, it was not only religion that was important, but rite and ritual, as well. We spoke in church only in whispers and were never allowed to kneel with our butts against the pew as others did. We stood when we were supposed to, knelt when the program said to, made the sign of the cross over ourselves in different ways at various times during the service – everything in accordance with carefully crafted rules and guidelines. Our brand of religion was highly regimented. And now, I saw her letting her grip slip on all that ceremony in favor of something completely different – a fiery and flamboyant and freestyle form of faith aimed clearly more at the gut than at the mind or heart. Looking at her then and seeing her attention focused so keenly on the charismatic TV preacher told me that something very different was taking place in her spiritual universe.

I used the moment as an opportunity to excuse myself to visit the coffee bar and stretch my legs. As I left the room, I heard the volume go up.

When I returned, the program was over and the TV was off. And so I decided to ask her more about this new twist in her faith. I asked her if she still felt the same about the picturesque little white-painted Episcopal Church our family had attended for years. A wealthy area rancher had built tiny St. John's a century earlier as a wedding gift for his new bride, a prim and proper Anglican from New England who had begrudgingly followed him to the unsophisticated coastal prairie of South Texas. The church was as quaint as a postcard and had been a cornerstone of our family's faith for more than twenty-five years. I had been married there, both of my children were baptized there, and the courtyard held a rose-filled peace garden and bell tower dedicated to my brother. Both she and my father had served in a variety of posts on the vestry.

"It's fine," she said. "But it's barely hanging on." We had discussed this before. There are many small towns in South Texas that have aging Episcopal congregations. But there are fewer clergymen than there are churches, so local leadership and worship have fallen largely to laypersons – like my father – who conduct simple Morning Prayer services for ever-smaller audiences, and to "circuit-rider" priests who often conduct as many as three communion services in separate communities on any given Sunday. We talked about the local parishioners – people we had known for decades.

"Any new faces?" I asked.

"Not really," she said. "We get an occasional young couple or a new family every once in a while, but most of them move on to something else."

"Any idea why?"

"We don't have as much to offer. They're looking for something bigger – something more exciting – something for the kids."

"So where do they go?"

"They're driving all the way to Houston – to go to the megachurches."

Ah, megachurches. I knew something about them. Living in the largely conservative, evangelical outskirts of Dallas as I have for more than two decades, I am surrounded by some of the largest and most well-known megachurches in America. I live amongst the people – and count them among my friends, neighbors and work associates – who make up the throngs of membership. I get caught up in the traffic snarls that tie up local streets every Saturday evening and Sunday morning. And my mailbox gets clogged with the slick, expensive marketing materials – always with the pastor's smiling face emblazoned across the front – announcing the launch of some amazing new program that is sure to make my life happier, more meaningful and more fulfilled.

Small conventional churches of all denominations – once vital cornerstones of every community – are facing hard times these days, with membership either flat or declining in most areas. Some faiths have launched expensive national advertising campaigns to show their relevance and inclusiveness in hopes of attracting more of the growing young families that are prime recruits for all churches. They launch creative new programs to make the idea of going to worship fun and enticing. They freshen up their images to appear more youthful and vital and dynamic. But just as small stores on every town square in America are ceding the consumer battle to the big-box retailers out by the highway, today's older, traditional churches are rapidly losing ground to the cultural phenomenon of the megachurch.

Denominations like the Episcopal Church do not help their cause by bogging themselves down in divisive issues like which prayer book to use, or whether women should be admitted to the priesthood, or if gays should be granted civil unions or even welcomed into the church body. Catholics fuss over the Vatican II protocols and struggle with whether it's okay to eat meat on Fridays. Even Baptists have split themselves into conservatives versus ultra-conservatives over statement-of-faith issues like a wife's submission to her husband's "servant leadership." And while all of this happens, the megachurches – offering up non-denominational simplicity, variety and convenience – gobble up the spoils.

My children and I had the opportunity, several years ago, to attend a megachurch several times as guests of a friend. On the whole, it was an experience not to be forgotten. On our first visit, we were met at the entrance to the football-stadium sized parking lot by a vest-clad member of the *Parking Ministry,* who guided us to a special parking area right up front reserved for visitors, where we encountered a smiling, badge-wearing representative of the *New Member Ministry.* From there we were led into the shiny, corporate headquarters-looking building and handed over to the staff of the *Administration Ministry,* who stuffed our arms with brochures and gathered our names and other personal data before handing us off to the *Ushering Ministry* who, as expected, led us down to the very front rows of the coliseum-sized auditorium, where we were immediately swarmed and glad-handed by a dozen overly happy members of the *"Oh, you're just going to love this" Ministry.*

On the way through the process, we walked past bookstores and coffee bars and even a food court, and signs that pointed the way to a dozen other ministries targeted to youth groups of all ages, the elderly, the single, the bereaved, and more. No sooner had we nestled into our comfortable, theater-style seats than we were on our feet again, presented with an amazingly polished professional rock show – fifteen minutes of dazzling lights, thumping beats, skillful musicianship and a quartet of high-energy singers, all choreographed in lock-step to praise music lyrics emblazoned across a trio of drive-in-movie-sized projection screens hanging high overhead.

As the music built to a crescendo and then a thundering climax, the lights shifted to center stage and out walked the true star of the show – the pastor. It is no exaggeration to say that today's megachurch pastors are true celebrities. They make millions selling books and by doing radio programs, telecasts and even tours to other megachurches. They live in high style with limousines and vacation homes and are tended to by flocks of assistant pastors, stylists and handlers. They are also bona fide stars because they are truly gifted at what they do. They are masterful at creating entertaining and enlightening links between fundamentalist scriptures and the post-modern world of soccer games and suburbia. And they are master promoters, too.

During her junior high years, my daughter was invited by friends to attend a weeknight teen event at a nearby mega-church – a giant "Welcome to Worship!" sign was planted in our front yard before she even returned home. On another evening, she won a shiny new ten-speed bicycle. I never figured out the link between seeking spirituality and winning prizes, but we dubbed the new bike the "Jesus wheels" and offered it to a youngster down the block who needed it more than we did. The whole concept seemed more like a circus to me than anything I might have thought of as religion.

But my mother was right. There is an awful lot about these institutions that is appealing to overstretched suburban families who struggle with an endless list of work and family commitments and find it amazingly easy to show up for an hour of *religiotainment* on Sunday morning and then neatly check off the box marked "faith" on their busy family to-do lists. This mass marketing of feel-good religion is allowed to flourish because we, as consumers, allow it to. More than that, we demand it. In a world that thrives on convenience, it simply makes great sense to pack our need for spirituality and a greater understanding of God in along with our craving for lower prices and broader selection. We've enabled an entirely new brand of religion to sprout up side-by-side with thirty-screen cinemas and big-box retailers. We've made God as easy and accessible as Walmart or the Home Depot.

The phenomenon of the megachurch has grown in tandem with the rise of evangelicalism in America – one fueling the other. They have thrived by using excitement, enthusiasm and entertainment to gobble up a sizeable portion of the population that is "unchurched" – a term that, in the megachurch vernacular, applies to anyone who hasn't been reborn in their evangelical way. And they have also flourished by cannibalizing from the many thousands of traditional corner church congregations that simply can't compete with the variety, convenience, size and scope of what these religious mega-malls have to offer.

The problem I have with this is that megachurches, with virtually no exception, are completely structured around the spiritual, cultural and social vision of the single charismatic personality that owns center stage. Which means that, in essence, many of the most critical issues we face as humans are filtered through the minds of a select few individuals and then disseminated back out to the hearts and minds of millions of willing and eager consumers as the literal Gospel truth. Think of an hourglass, with a world of issues funneling down through its aperture into a single strand of thought that lands back down on top of all of us. Megapastors become the gatekeepers for what is right and wrong, true or false, good or evil, and real or imagined – in not just the spiritual world, but also in the larger realm of society as a whole. They alone tell us how God works and how the world works and how they believe we are to conform our lives to both.

When we attend a megachurch, we basically agree to accept the singular mindset of that individual. Pop-star megapastors have the freedom and the power to speak about whatever strikes their fancy – their own worldview – and are accountable to no one. We allow the powerful dynamics of lights, music and charismatic entertainment to take the place of our own ability to ask, evaluate and analyze the true nature of spirituality, simply because it's fast, easy and convenient. In perhaps the ultimate irony, megapastors consistently drive home the point that we need to develop a personal relationship with God to achieve salvation, yet they are the ones who define not only God, but how our personal relationship should work, as well. We eagerly permit them to insert themselves as an extra link in a chain that should never have more than two links: *God and us.*

And so I see challenges at both ends of the church spectrum. The small town corner churches of Norman Rockwell's Christmas cards have failed to change and modernize, anchoring themselves in traditions that mean less and less when measured by the yardstick of man's changing interaction with the world. And megachurches – driven by powerful religious individuals – have gone to the other extreme, changing the entire spiritual experience to meet the momentary needs of modern pop culture. This leaves a large void in the middle for a growing set of enlightened seekers who want much of what all of religion has to offer, but want it packaged with far more reason, relevance, intelligence and depth – and far less zealotry.

This may be a far-reaching macro-statement, but I sense that we could be on the cusp of a new Age of Enlightenment in religion. Not merely a cultural shift – like creating megachurches that simply mirror "bigger is better" consumer trends. But a more universal and fundamental rethinking of religion that may take place over the next hundred years or so that will combine the very best of the traditions and heritage of our ancient faiths with a newer, more up-to-date and realistic understanding of what the idea of God can and should mean to our world. I believe that the cult of the megachurch is little more than a fad that will self-implode over the next few decades. It is the natural cycle of things. History has shown that institutions built around the all-too-human frailties of men and women are wont to do that. Power is a narcotic that leads men to fall, and we see these dynasties tumble almost on a monthly basis. Take away the powerful and solitary leader, and most megachurches would eventually scatter and die, like a beehive deprived of its queen.

Just as mom and pop stores are beginning to reappear on the city square, churchgoers may again set out to find the intimacy and closeness of something smaller – something deeper and more personally meaningful. In the early centuries of Christianity, before Emperor Theodosius I made it the official religion of Rome and established Jesus as a deity – a real-life God on Earth – the faith was simply known as *The Way*. It existed as an underground network of small groups that met privately to break bread – intimately and spiritually – in homes. The understanding of the life and teachings of Jesus was deeply personal – a faith to be shared and owned by small gatherings of individuals, often under penalty of death. No latte, no praise bands, no Easter Bunny, no Christmas cards – just a purely personal focus on spirituality. Maybe religion will find itself returning to those roots. I would like to live to see that. I could buy into something like *The Way*.

As my mother progressed month-by-month toward the end of her life, she drew ever closer to the faith she had followed from youth. I think this is normal; as we come to the realization that we will soon be face to face with whatever God we have known, we are left with no option but to strengthen our beliefs any way that we can. At the very least, we are forced to address the issues of faith and God more directly, more sharply, and more inquisitively. I recognized my mother's need to explore all avenues to faith – even big-haired TV preachers. I wanted her to grip tightly to what she believed. It worked for her and, because of that, it was right for her. I greatly admired her faith.

We spent the balance of the afternoon talking about other things, covering the gamut from broad family memories to the details of what she liked for dinner on the hospital menu. We laughed and shared and generally enjoyed the deep connection that only sons and mothers can know.

Before I left, I glanced back up at the TV – now tuned to some innocuous talk show – and asked her if she really thought it made a difference – how we prayed, who we followed, what we believed. She leaned over to look at me with her one good eye and paused, thinking.

"We'll see," she said. "We shall see."

ELEVEN: CAB FARE

There was an occasion many years ago, when I was still married to my first wife, that she made a business trip that brought her back home early on a Sunday morning. I believe the trip was to a convention in Las Vegas, so I'm sure she was returning home with nothing but lint in her pockets. She did have a twenty-dollar bill, which she'd wisely hidden in her purse in order to pay for a cab ride home. Smart thinking. However, being early on a Sunday morning, the cab driver – a recent immigrant of Middle Eastern descent – who collected her at the airport and deposited her at our home a few short miles away had apparently just started out for the day and had no change. What happened when they arrived at the curb in front of the house was part clash of cultures, part mismanaged financial transaction, and part plain old misunderstanding. No doubt religious perceptions may have played a role.

My former wife is a fine person with a deep love of people and a heart of gold. But like many of us, she also has the ability, when all the stars and planets are just in the perfect sort of misalignment, to get mildly indignant in the face of a perceived slight. And when the cabbie explained to her over and over again that he didn't have any change for her single twenty-dollar bill, I think she perhaps suspected – like many of us might – that the cabbie was pulling a fast one. After a bit of heated discussion, she simply handed over her Andrew Jackson and stormed into the house. *Trip over.*

The next day when I went out to check the mail, I discovered an envelope wedged between the doorknob and doorframe. I could feel something inside but there was nothing written on the outside. I gathered it up with the rest of the mail and brought it in. When I opened it up I found a crisp twenty-dollar bill and a printed pamphlet that outlined the basic beliefs of Islam. I had heard all about the story of the taxi ride from the morning before, so I realized immediately that the envelope had been left by the anonymous cab driver. My curiosity sparked, I sat down and scanned through the brochure, which described in broad detail the five pillars of the Islamic faith. It made me think back almost instantly to a fundraising brochure I had done several years earlier for a local Jewish congregation. That brochure had been built around the three pillars of that faith – *Torah* (lifelong learning), *Avodah* (worship) and *Gemilut Chasadim* (good deeds). Glancing quickly at the five pillars of Islam, it didn't take long to see the differences.

The five pillars of Islam – the belief that there is but one God and Mohammad is his prophet; communal ritual prayer, five times each day; fasting during the lunar month of Ramadan; an obligatory annual giving of alms following Ramadan; and, for those able to do so, the requirement to make a pilgrimage to Mecca at least once in their lifetime – seemed, at face value, as opposite as night from day to the columns that propped up the Jewish faith. But then I started to read further and common themes began to emerge. Dicing them down, I could see that both traditions placed a great emphasis on faith at the personal level, but also in the strength and value of community. Almost directly, each faith put forth a requirement to visit charity upon the less fortunate. And in general ways, each faith presented its beliefs as a complete way of life – not just a convenient set of rules or recommendations to follow.

Christians like numerical structure, too. And while I hadn't run across any specific list of pillars in Christianity, I knew of at least two statements of faith – the Nicene Creed and the Apostles' Creed – that performed much the same function, establishing a column-like foundation for the ways we should live and believe.

Looking more deeply at the tract the cab driver had left, I saw that everyday guidelines for living – built around qualities like honesty, integrity, respect, fairness and dignity – were featured prominently throughout the faith pillars. Indeed, one paragraph seemed to point directly to why the cab driver had gone who-knows-how-far out of his way to leave us his hard-earned twenty dollar bill; the values of honesty and honor far outweighed the value of the currency in question.

I've never forgotten that incident. And even when the calamitous events of 9/11 happened, and our country was suddenly shot through with a wave of anti-Muslim feelings and a deep mistrust of any religion largely not understood here, I managed to hold on to the idea that this man showed by example how God's basic principles are as fundamental to his native Islam as they are to Christianity, or Hinduism, or Judaism or Buddhism. When we scrape away all the fundamentalist fear and ignorance-driven propaganda that divide us from our brothers and sisters of all beliefs, we find that we do basically – and truly – all aim for the same things in this Earthly existence.

The reason that I bring up this story is to highlight the idea that we, as a society, have largely lost our ability to look at religious pluralism with open, accepting and objective eyes. And we have also partly lost our willingness to discuss – openly and honestly – ideas about religion that can lead us all to a greater understanding of the Almighty's intentions and our purpose here in the Earthly realm. Religion has become such a loaded and toxic topic that we all immediately gird ourselves to defend our beliefs quickly when the subject comes up or, worse still, we move over to the offensive and go overboard to persuade others of our own very correct ideas. At the root of it all, religion is a very personal fundamental belief for each of us. We'll all take a stand for what we believe – it's as vital a component of our identity as our hair color or skin tone. And thank God that we, as a society, have taken to heart the old admonishment to not discuss religion in public – or at least many of us have. It's probably the only way we can get along peaceably with some semblance of a civil society. We've learned to keep that monster tamed, at least well enough to all share roadways and office spaces.

For many people these days, to have any sort of open religious dialogue is about the same as pulling the pin from a hand grenade and playing a game of catch. The discussion will lob along painlessly enough for a while, and then go *boom.* There will virtually always be an explosion of some sort, even among close friends and family. Sometimes *especially* among friends and family.

In my view, religion is becoming increasingly polarized at precisely the time when we need more open discussion, more free analysis, more honest evaluation and more common understanding. We need to unplant our heels and be truly willing to listen to other points of view. We need to feel free to ask open, honest and challenging questions. No matter how well we think we are playing with others in the world's giant sandbox, it's still largely a story of us against them. This goes on between religions and within religions. In fact, it has almost become a *defining component* of religion.

In the months following 9/11, much effort was made all across the Western world to show solidarity and spiritual collaboration between faiths. There were – probably still are, at least in the spirit of lip-service – public gatherings that brought together leaders from Christianity, Judaism and Islam to promote the common understanding and shared beliefs of monotheism. I remember that our local city government welcomed a variety of clergy to come and say opening prayers for city council meetings – at least until a Wiccan priest signed up to participate. I think these efforts at unification have been largely welcomed and successful. If nothing else, they are refreshing to see.

But, in practical reality, one could always feel some underlying tension in these gatherings. Each religion has, at its core, a fundamental belief that it alone possesses the one true path to God. There are statements of faith within each that, in fact, clearly say so. So these multi-religion gatherings are always tempered by the fact that spiritual disharmony – even among pastoral friends who simply wear different ceremonial hats – is always just a scratch below the surface. We can all talk pleasantly about the oneness of man and our quest for the common good, but as for how we reach Heaven, that's a subject that's better left untouched. That's the big elephant in the middle of the room that nobody wants to mention.

In the worlds of anthropology and sociology, we explore the basic human ideas that people pretty much hang out with other people like themselves. It's a tribal thing that goes back to the dawn of man. There's some small part of every human that distrusts those things or people that are foreign to us. We all have some tiny fear of what we don't fully know or understand, no matter how much we wish to deny the fact. And I think this is one of the root causes of the tension that exists in the world of religion today. Combined with the immediacy of communications – television, the Internet, e-mail – we're all exposed to those sensitive differences more and more. Thus, the rise in insecurities between people of all faiths; our differences are more exposed and obvious. Of course, this is a broad and dangerous generalization that I've made; we all know that there are enlightened people within all faiths who have the ability to step above the dogma to embrace the love and teachings of all – after all, we simply must agree that the universal truths that lie at the foundations of every major faith are not only similar but, as the cabbie's brochure helped to explain, virtually identical.

Seveal years ago, Karen Armstrong, the one-time aspiring Catholic nun and author of many in-depth books on religion including the benchmark *A History of God,* traveled through Dallas on a book tour and sat down to an interview with the religion writers at the local major daily newspaper. I've read much of what she's written and find her amazingly progressive in her thoughts and ideas. It should be obvious to all that she is a spiritual seeker in the truest sense of the word. But while her brand of intellectual curiosity is perfectly acceptable in places like New York or London, it doesn't always go over so well out here in the Heartland.

In the question-and-answer feature, Ms. Armstrong addressed the issue of an "impersonal" God. By which, she meant to describe the notion that God is not a person – but an idea, a higher-level entity, something that we're not supposed to truly understand or recognize in the human sense; *God is something that transcends mere humanity.* It all seemed clear and rational to me. But I think the reporter never got past the initial mention of the word "impersonal," hanging up somewhere on the idea that Ms. Armstrong was implying that we're not supposed to have a direct, personal relationship with God. It was a classic case of intellectualism meeting protestant evangelicalism – not exactly well-suited bedfellows. And the balance of the interview beyond that point took a decidedly downward spin. The letters to the editor that ran in following weeks read from bad to worse. Ms. Armstrong had clearly not struck her marvelous chord of spiritual understanding here in the buckle of the Bible Belt.

Of course, the real meaning of what she was saying was anything but the notion that we're not supposed to have a deep, personal connection to the God who created us. To the inquiring mind, everything in all of her work points to the thought that our greatest task in life is to seek and strive to become ever closer to the God of our understanding. But, humans being what we are, we allow our natural distrust for alternative views or opinions to get the better of us and preemptively cloud our ability to listen and judge with reason. Out here in the red-state region of big-haired preachers and megachurches, Ms. Armstrong might as well have been speaking Klingon. I still feel pain for her, although I'm sure she's faced similar misunderstandings with the media in other regions and among other audiences. That would come with her turf – and working as she does to push the envelope of spiritual exploration can't always be easy. I hope that some day she'll swing back through. True seekers should read her books.

But every small moment of conflict that bubbles up through our larger discussion of religion – even minor ones like Ms. Armstrong's brush with the religious right (their new mantra: "we're both religious and right") – helps to stir up the issues that can ultimately lead to broadened understanding. The more we raise the topics, even in disagreement, the more opportunities we create for progress. While some of us may think that God has stopped talking, that's no reason why we humans should – we should constructively be jabbering up a storm. There is no one single definition of God that works for everybody. Nor should there be. No one is right, and no one is wrong. If the God that works for you happens to sync up with the God of pop culture or history or your upbringing or the local megachurch, then that's fine and wonderful. If it doesn't, that's okay, too. I believe that God is an idea – one that deserves the very best of our naturally inquisitive minds. We can and should seek out and find counsel and opinion – honest curiosity is our key to discovery. As Jesus said, *knock and the door will be opened unto you; seek and you shall find.*

The greatest thinkers in human history – the DaVincis and the Newtons who helped to move humankind forward by small steps – did little more than ask the open-ended question *why?* And then kept on asking and asking and asking some more until they arrived at some conclusion or developed a new idea or gizmo that led to a new rung on our shared ladder of learning. I think the key to providing greater harmony between religious – and even non-religious – believers of every flavor all around the globe rests with honest inquiry instead of closed-minded condemnation. This will serve to create links of sameness instead of severing common threads – and that is vital if we are to revamp religion to provide the relevant foundation it needs to be for our collective future.

My family moved to Mississippi right at the tail end of what history defines as the Civil Rights Era. As a fifth-grader, it jumped out at me that there were still separate fountains in the hallways of my school. Even though the signs reading *black only* or *white only* had been removed, I could see the shadows on the wall where they had once been. The school buildings themselves were as different as day and night – it was easy to tell which had been reserved for whites or which for blacks. Having come from West Texas, the cultural mood of the Deep South was new and different, as was the experience of being around black kids, who made up a solid fifty percent of my school. Being fifth-graders, we saw no difference in each other. We were kids and not much else mattered – even as the school bus we rode made stops at shacks and shanties on swampy dirt lanes en route to the middle-class neighborhoods where most white kids lived.

I did notice something different, however, when my mother took me to sign up for Little League baseball. The only game in town was the Dixie Youth League and, as the name might imply, it was for white boys only. I recall thinking it odd that the boys with whom I sat side-by-side in my classrooms were nowhere to be seen around the playing fields. My mother was incensed. At the first parents' meeting, she rose – as a complete newcomer in a small town dominated by families with generational roots that went back to before the Civil War – and voiced her concern, loudly and firmly. She asked why? *Why were little black boys not allowed to play in the town's only league?*

Although I never felt the wrath of her actions on the playing field, I know that she faced a great deal of quiet condemnation around the community – an unspoken disdain that lasted at least to some degree for the duration of our years there. Looking back, I admire her willingness to challenge the status quo. It must have taken some guts. And, while nothing changed in the league during the time that I played there, a crack eventually did form in the dike of an out-of-date institution that was quite unwilling to change on its own. Within a few years, the league made the inevitable leap to full integration.

I don't claim that my mother single handedly brought about a long-overdue change in the baseball program of a backwater southern town. I can't say that her actions started the ball rolling. But what she did took courage and did perhaps point the way for other voices that began to rise together to create the change that did ultimately come. Like the DaVincis and Newtons before her, she had the courage to ask why? And then to keep asking until the question became too obvious to ignore. One small voice is enough, over time, to create great change. Each of us has the ability and the obligation to stand on our principles and ask why? And then work to demonstrate the basic ideas behind our faith – behind all faiths – instead of focusing only on our outward definitions. By doing so, we help to highlight our similarities and make our differences smaller and weaker, until they eventually fade away. And, along with that comes the equally important commitment to listen open-mindedly to what others have to share.

My immediate neighbors for the past several years are Muslims – a rare and wonderful luck-of-the-draw for my family in our largely homogenous white, Christian suburban neighborhood. They have been, without doubt, some of the finest people I have ever met – gracious, inviting and courteous almost to a fault. They came to introduce themselves even before we had the opportunity to pay the customary welcoming visit to them. They continue to bring us gifts from their garden, and have never once missed the chance to shake hands, smile and engage in pleasant conversation. Faith – *theirs or ours* – has never been a topic of discussion. A year ago we received an invitation to their daughter's wedding, which we gladly accepted – we view each opportunity to experience the celebrations of other faiths as a chance to learn. The festival of marriage took place over the course of several days, culminating with an extravagant dinner – a *valima* – attended by perhaps a thousand people, nearly all of whom were Muslims, many visiting from other countries. It was interesting to be among the small handful of non-Muslims in attendance – a rare chance to experience the sense of what minorities must feel in our culture every day. Far from feeling segregated as outsiders, we were welcomed as honored guests.

After hours of socializing, the broad walls of the ballroom were drawn back to reveal two huge and lavish buffet lines, one of which we duly joined. I was nearly through the line – with my wife, son and daughter – when

I realized that my line was made up almost exclusively of women and young children; the men and older boys were all in the other line. Thus, we were introduced to an everyday Muslim tradition that we had not known. A few grins came our way as we acknowledged our little cultural *faux pas,* but we were never made to feel uncomfortable. We learned, grew and enjoyed the experience.

But the incident started me thinking about faith and culture and the little ways that we are all different. And I came to realize that what we might refer to as differences between faiths are in essence nothing more than differences between customs and traditions. If, as the common links between pillars of the faith show, our beliefs and rules for living are much the same, then it simply must be the external wrappings of religion – the ways we put our faith into practice within the context of the cultures in which we live – that make up the bulk of what we see as dissimilar. As belief in God – really all of religion – has sprouted and grown over the past five thousand years of humanity's rise to dominance on the planet, it has been defined by the minutiae of how it exists at the local level far more than it has been defined by the beliefs that lie at its common core. If we look at the shared desire to live our lives fairly, treat others with dignity, take care of our less-fortunate brethren, and create strong bonds that strengthen families and communities, then *we are all of the same faith, are we not?*

The big snag in all of this is, of course, religious extremism – of all types. There are simply zealots of every ilk who are so locked into the "my way is the only way and all others must be converted or perish" mentality, that it may well be impossible to ever envision a religious world where our differences are not highlighted more than our similarities. There will always be those whose sole intent is to foment divisiveness, who can never see the many things that all men share in common over the small-minded belief that they alone possess the keys to the kingdom.

Many corporations these days realize the benefits to be gained by putting groups of diverse people through team-building exercises like a "ropes" course. One of the more extreme of these training groups buys old America's Cup yachts and teaches executives and managers the precision team working skills needed to work together toward a common goal in the fast-paced and challenging world of open-ocean racing (if anybody is short a team member, please look me up). I've often thought it would be an interesting exercise to take the extremists from all the major religions and sign them up for one of these courses. Or put them together as a group on a deserted island – call it *Survivor Religious Extremist* – and leave them alone for a while. Make them work together. Let them learn more about each other as people. Show them they must learn to cooperate in order to succeed.

They would either kill each other – which I doubt – or come away from the experience with a common bond and understanding that, while we may each be different in the specifics of our natures and ways, we truly need each other's care, support, love and encouragement to survive. Better still, we can use the very perspectives that make us unique to enhance our own worldviews – to grow and learn by seeing faith and God through the eyes of others. It's easy to stand back from afar and say things that are hateful and hurtful and designed to generate fear and distrust about someone who is different from us. It's much more difficult – or downright impossible – to say or do those things when we stand face to face.

Simply put, if we spent less time trying to convert each other, and more time trying to understand each other – looking for those things that are similar in our beliefs instead of those things that are different – we might eventually find ourselves standing at the threshold of a marvelous, unified global faith. Imagine that – the power of people everywhere in a single quest for spiritual understanding – recognizing the need to respect and celebrate the unique differences of our cultures, customs and traditions – merging as one atop the universal common denominator of God.

That's a pretty big idea, I think. Not bad for the cost of a taxi ride.

Twelve: Wheels in Motion

I was working in my office at the front of my house one fine afternoon and staring out the window – as advertising writers who get paid an embarrassing amount of money to write a one-page ad are often prone to do – when I had the marvelous opportunity to watch a neighbor who lived across the cul-de-sac teaching his son to ride a bicycle without training wheels. The little boy – then perhaps six years old – had been pedaling around the neighborhood for months on the bike with the added benefit of the training wheels, but now it was time to move beyond that. It was time to learn and grow.

For the boy, it was time to develop a faith – of sorts. It was time to go through the fear and uncertainty of change to discover a new world that existed beyond – a time to try the untried. So dad had removed the training wheels and

– we all know this drill – was gingerly supporting the boy with both hands and gently coasting him first a few feet, then a few yards at a time down the driveway and out toward the cul-de-sac. The kid was terrified. Apparently he knew beyond a shadow of a doubt that the bike would stand up safely and move along securely on four wheels. It would stand up on its own just like a table. No leaning, no tilting, no falling over. But with two wheels removed, how could it? Even a six-year-old mind knows that, with the kickstand up, a two-wheeled bicycle, released from the hand's grip and left alone to the law of gravity, would instantly and surely fall over. And now this young lad was being urged, prodded and tenderly reassured by a loving dad that the bicycle – now clipped of its supporting training wheels – would, in fact, ride along on its own and remain upright.

Time and time again – perhaps a dozen or twenty times altogether – the father rolled the son down the driveway, moving slightly farther and faster each time. On each occasion, the boy coasted a few feet more down the pavement before inevitably closing his eyes, releasing his grip on the handlebars and pancaking over on one side. I admired the boy's willingness to continue, over and over again. Thank God for helmets and elbow pads.

But while this young boy had lots of grit and staying power – he was one of those freckle-nosed kids whom you just know will grow up to be a fearless, natural athlete – what he lacked was faith. He lacked the trust and commitment to believe that what his father was telling him – that his beloved four-wheeler would operate even more effectively as a two-wheeler – could ever be true. At face value, it went against every grain of his being, defying every little thing he believed he knew about the world.

And such is the nature of faith. We often fail to believe in what we cannot see or feel. We find it impossible to go against our own natural, human intuition – what we have witnessed with our own eyes or felt with our own hands. We think we understand one way that the world will operate – the single way that life will work for us and around us – and we fail to consider that there could easily be an altogether different *modus operandi*. We fail to trust that there may be unseen forces about us that can operate in an entirely new way. A spiritual way – *the way of faith.*

This is not a simple story about learning to trust. It's way more than that, for trust and faith can be different things. I can trust that if I have an appointment to meet with someone at 10 a.m. for coffee, they will most likely – if they are any sort of trustworthy person at all – be there. Trust is Faith Junior. To have faith is to go much farther out on a limb and believe that some unknown or unforeseen or little-understood power can and will do things that we often do not expect. In some instances, say, with the little boy on the bike, the expectation can be very small or nothing at all. We simply have no reason to think that something based on faith alone will happen. But faith defies the physical laws of the real world we see around us.

What the little boy on the bicycle failed to realize is that there is a miraculous power that comes into play when riding a bicycle that we cannot see, feel or – to six-year-olds – even comprehend. It's called centrifugal force. And it's one of those quirky laws of nature that maybe Isaac Newton fully understood – but I certainly don't – that says an object in motion will strive to stay in motion and in the same position relative to the world around it. It's the force that keeps a top standing upright as it spins on its tiny tip. And it's the force that will easily keep a bicycle – even a unicycle – standing up straight and sturdy on its very own. As long as a wheel is spinning. Stop the bike and – in keeping with the little boy's limited view of physics – it will surely fall over.

Centrifugal force is the amazing invisible power behind the gyroscope. I had a toy gyro as a kid and would pull the string to set the disk spinning and then marvel at the force of resistance as I tried to move it side to side. High-tech versions of the same simple device do everything from keeping spacecrafts on course to helping people with damaged nervous systems maintain balance. I can watch a gyro spin and feel the physical effect of what it does, but I have no clue as to what makes it work. Stop the spin, like the wheels on the boy's bike, and the magic goes away.

The bike story, of course, has a happy ending. It's a good thing and one of those comforting facts of life in the world that fathers are generally successful in teaching children to ride bicycles. There is always an epiphany, an instant when the slightest hint of faith overtakes the last ounce of hesitation, and the miracle happens. As I watched the boy and the father, I witnessed that moment for myself, and a smile undoubtedly came across my face as I saw the little boy make the extra effort to lean against the falling bicycle on this umpteenth try and thereby urge the vehicle on for an additional few wobbly meters. I could pinpoint the instant in the boy's life when he first realized that this could work for him. I saw the bulb flicker. And then grow brighter. He did something that at first felt alien – and then became quite natural. He began to believe.

Within days, the boy was a terror in the cul-de-sac, jumping curbs and leaning over the way speedway motorcycle racers do in tight turns to follow the curves of the sidewalk as it arced its way from house to house around the circle. His life would never be the same. He had learned that forces we cannot see or feel could do things in our lives that we simply can't fully comprehend on our own. He had developed faith in something bigger and more powerful than himself. And he didn't even need to understand it. It simply worked.

We have all experienced this epiphany at some point during our lives. We look high above our heads and watch airplanes that weigh perhaps a half a million pounds or more soar up into the sky. We see ships made of steel that weigh hundreds of thousands of tons float on the top of the water without sinking. We wonder, *why do these things work?* There are scientific explanations, of course; in the case of an airplane, Bernoulli's Principle comes into play, which states that air moving faster over the curved top of a wing creates negative pressure – a vacuum – that actually lifts the craft into the sky. In the case of floating ships, it's all about the displacement of water – the amount of sea that a sealed ship's hull keeps out of the vessel as gravity pushes it down weighs more than the ship itself. But in both cases, these are things that by initial reason or appearance should not occur. Heavier-than-air planes should not fly and boats made of iron should not float in water – at least to little boys. But they do.

In my experience, faith that works is something that has to be acquired, usually through lots of blind effort. It does not come naturally. It doesn't come through prayer – although that's certainly a big part of it. It comes by trusting and by doing. It comes by gaining the willingness to put one small foot – even just the toe on the end of that small foot – out into the unknown and believing that there will be some outcome that we perhaps cannot predict and certainly cannot control. We do not have to understand; in fact, it's better – probably easier – if we don't. We get pushed and prodded by life's events into situations where willingness comes much faster and easier than it would at other times. We find ourselves in situations where trying the same approach over and over again simply will not work; we need to find a new way. We have to be willing to try something different – in hopes that we may find a different outcome.

I think back to my own youthful years playing Little League baseball. Never a gifted athlete, I spent most games rotating between left field and the bench. I played because that's what the boys in my neighborhood did – and because all teams need benchwarmers. Although I made an occasional walk around the bases and moved up to play third base on the rare occasion that we were up by a hefty score, there was never any secret amongst my teammates that my personal strengths lay far away from the diamond.

In my final year of play, my team got a brand-new coach just as the season began. He was a complete newcomer – not one of the regular gang of dads whose sons were pitchers and who knew the individual skills – or lack thereof – of every boy in the league. As our new coach set out to drill the team, he cast aside any preconceived notions about any of us – we all started out with a fresh slate. He would rebuild the team to his own liking from scratch. And this included a fresh review of our batting skills. When it was my turn to step up to the plate and show my lack-of-stuff, this new coach never displayed any sign of doubt as to my batting ability. He simply waited for me to hit the ball. As was my habit, I missed the first, second and third pitches tossed my way. As I prepared to set the bat down and return to the dugout – as was also my habit – he called me back to the plate where he knelt down and discussed with me, in detail, the art of hitting a baseball. He walked me through my swing, and he helped me set my feet at the right angles and bend my knees just so. In short, he coached me.

But most important, he told me that the secret to connecting with any pitch was to *keep my eye on the ball.* No matter what, no matter how fast, whether curve ball or slider or sinker or knuckleball, he admonished me to keep my eye on the ball. He explained to me that if I could do that, then my body would do the rest. He assured me that there was some unexplainable physical connection between my eyes, my brain, my shoulders and arms, and the bat that would work its magic if I allowed it to. He explained to me that I didn't have to understand how it worked, but only that it did. I decided to give it a try.

I do not recall who was more surprised – me or the team of boys milling about in the field kicking anthills and picking dandelions – when my bat impacted the ball with a resounding crack and knocked it way out over second base. The coach called for another pitch, and then another, and I smacked into them both. By now, the boys in the field had rejoined the game. They were fielding balls that I had hit. One after another, I tracked the round white objects that streaked from the pitcher's flinging arm with my eyes and pounded them back out into the field.

By the end of the season, I held the best batting record on the team. I moved from benchwarmer and occasional left fielder, batting ninth on the lineup, to the "clean-up" slot at number four. I developed the ability to put the ball anywhere I wanted to in the field and racked up an impressive runs-batted-in stat. As a result of new confidence at the plate, my play in the field improved, too. I never became the kind of athlete who achieved success without effort – I have always had to work hard at everything I do – but I finished my youth baseball career feeling satisfied with my labors. I also learned a wee-small bit about believing in things I could not understand.

I didn't see faith the day it showed up to work in my adult life. I flat out didn't know that it was coming. I can't show anybody a date on the calendar that's marked *this is the day that I discovered faith in something greater than me.* It's just not there. But I can generally look back at a time in my life, several years into recovery, when I genuinely started taking steps that I wouldn't have taken before. Steps in faith. I had reached a place where operating on self-propulsion had taken me as far as I could go. I was ready for a change, for something new. I had little to lose.

With a wife recently laid off, a five-year-old daughter, a son just several months old, and a fair amount of debt, I quit my job. It was a nice, stable and fairly secure position.

No doubt I might still be there if I hadn't left – I know others with whom I worked at that time who stayed and continue to do the same thing. But I had reached a place where everything in that world was predictable and known to me. There was little challenge and virtually no opportunity to truly discover who I was and what I could do. I looked around and realized that I was no longer drinking and using drugs every day – something I could not have said for many, many years before getting sober – and began to understand that something was working in my life that had not been there before.

Like the little boy making those first tenuous attempts to control the wobble and accept that the bicycle could stand up on its own two wheels, I was experiencing my own revelation of faith. I was beginning to believe that if I was willing to take positive action in my life – doing the very best that I could – and trust the outcome to something that I couldn't touch, see or understand, then something new, different and perhaps even better might happen in my life. I was in for quite a ride – complete with bumps and bruises.

The issue still rages within religion over whether faith in and of itself does the trick, or whether we are also required to provide some effort – the works. I'll leave it to the theologians to battle that one out. I can tell you that I found a God that works by being willing to go to work myself. God met me halfway, and that's fine by me. In the run-up to quitting my job – against the advice of bosses, coworkers, pretty much everyone I knew – I developed a sense of energy, enthusiasm and excitement that I hadn't felt in many years. I set out with vigor to take bold actions that would pave the way for success. I sought out seasoned experts whom I greatly admired and pestered them until they agreed to have lunch with me. I badgered them with questions. I picked their brains for every tidbit of advice that I could get.

I read books and studied and worked out the pros and cons of everything – all on a big, worn and dog-eared yellow pad of paper. I started paying attention to the broader world of business all around me – not only major corporations, but also the many little mom-and-pop shops that fill every strip mall and corner shopping center. I realized that every one of these had involved somebody – at some point – having the courage to follow a dream and stick a foot out into the unknown in blind faith. And to trust in something undefined and unpredictable, while doing the hard hands-on work every day.

What I learned from a dozen mentors could pretty much be boiled down into three simple rules. First, be good at what you do – make the best use of the skills and talents with which you've been blessed. Second, get up out of bed each day and do everything you can to use those abilities to help solve somebody's problems in the world around you. Universally, these people whom I admired and trusted had all been very good at doing that. And, in the process, had become quite successful in their own ways.

And the third rule – which now seems quite obvious – is to rely upon some universal source of strength and guidance that we cannot see, feel, touch, smell, taste or define, but that is very real and powerful, nonetheless. The first day that I set out on my own as a writer – with a desk, telephone and used computer in a small room at the back of a friend's auto-repair shop – I showed up early and spent a quiet hour in meditation and prayer. I promised to come and work as hard as I could each day. I did not know for certain that I would be successful, but I believed that I could be. I did my best to put faith to work.

I've had ups and downs in the intervening fifteen years, but I certainly have never looked back or regretted my decision to strike out on my own. I find that when I've had the inevitable down cycle in business, the cause has generally been the result of my becoming worried or fearful or overly concerned about my own financial security. This is always a good cue for me to once again stop and meditate on the one true source of power that drives my life, and to refocus my efforts on helping to solve someone's problems. It always works out. My God always takes care of me – so long as I continue to show up and do the simple things that lie in front of me each day.

Perhaps the most practical example of how I used this powerful new force comes from a very real-world problem in my financial life. I know many who would say that it's an unwise thing to quit one's job to start a new venture without a few bucks in the bank. Perhaps they're right – but I didn't listen. Others told me that if you wait until all the conditions are perfect to undertake some bold new phase in life – having a family, starting a business – then you're likely to never do anything at all. I had been bitten by the bug of faith and was, at that point in my life, quite willing to jump through any darkened doorway headfirst, without question. So when the natural lag in paychecks hit me after hanging out my shingle – the days of steady paychecks were long gone – my bills began to mount. Steadily and heavily. I discovered that invoices often languished in piles on desks and that clients who promised to pay in thirty days sometimes took sixty, or ninety days, or even longer. It would be months before I had anything like a stable, predictable income – as if I've ever had anything at all like that in the years since.

But I continued – as I had promised to the God I knew at that point in my life – to show up every day and answer the phone and do the work that landed in front of me. And business did gradually begin to build. Still, my small-but-significant debt would not go away. In fact, like a snowball rolling downhill, it grew bigger – with delinquencies piling on additional fees and my ability to borrow money quickly disappearing. After several months, this financial burden became an overwhelming dark cloud that hovered over my life. I dreaded answering the phone. I hated going to the mailbox.

Yet faith remained. And I likewise continued to show up with a smile on my face and work hard to solve problems for my clients – even though I was increasingly living in financial fear, knowing not what to do to speed my cash flow or generate enough income to bandage the wounds that were slowly bleeding the life out of my family and my dreams. I believed – I had seen too many examples in my life of a God that worked – but I lacked the knowledge of what to do physically to keep up my end of the faith/works bargain. *My faith needed a plan of action.*

An answer presented itself in the form of a speaker I heard one night at a meeting – again, another story of the lesson waiting for the willing student. The man who spoke had been in a similar situation with both business and personal finances, and he described in just a few minutes how he overcame the problem. Faith was never mentioned specifically, but it was implied. I had not been willing to talk openly about my financial problems – pride and ego easily conspire against me in situations like these. But I had learned to recognize a solution when I saw one. And so I cornered the man after the meeting and asked if we could talk over coffee. He readily agreed, and we sat down to draw up a very specific plan.

First, I was to gather up every bill that sat in all the piles on my desk. I was to sort them out in stacks by creditor and throw away everything except the most recent statement. At once, my overwhelming pile of problems seemed smaller, easier to handle, a mere handful of letters. I had struggled under the delusion that I had to somehow come up with a massive solution with which to tackle a seemingly insurmountable problem. Looking at the small stack, my goal suddenly seemed achievable. Next I was to take a single sheet of paper and, line-by-line, write out to whom I owed money and how much. Next to that number I was to write down in the simplest of terms exactly what each creditor wanted of me – how much money would make them happy right now, today. Again, when I did this, the challenge was framed up in a way that I could easily accept. The numbers did not take my breath away as I had feared they would.

Third, I was to write down the name and phone number of each person I needed to contact in order to work out a payment plan that would reasonably satisfy everyone. And finally, I was to call each creditor and put the whole plan into action – it would be simple, I was assured. Foolproof. *A story with a happy ending.* Except in my mind I knew this last part would not work. Hearing the messages on my answering machine and reading the letters I had received in the mail, I was convinced that these people – all of them, collectively as a group – despised me and looked down on me and would never be reasonable with me in my vulnerable position. I was a dog who was down, and they were kickers. Vicious ones at that.

"Ah," said the man. "This is where faith comes in – *you do have a little faith, don't you?*" What could you possibly mean? I wondered. All these people seem so hostile, and they've made all these demands, and there's no way that I can possibly deliver everything they all want from me.

"I can believe all I want, and there's still no way that I can still make all these numbers work out with everyone," I said.

He smiled and leaned forward. "Do you have two phones in your house?" I told him that I did. "And two chairs?" Again I nodded yes.

"Then here's what you do." He went on to explain to me that, with every call, I should take the second phone and switch it on and place it in front of the second chair beside me. This additional extension would be for my God, or my higher power, or whatever other entity I might wish – who or what didn't matter. The idea was, quite simply, that I would not be making these calls alone. I would be making them with the help of some force that would support me and back me up and give me a sense of partnership. To carry the notion a step further, I was to only use the term "we" on my end of each conversation, and never the solo "I."

I easily laugh when I think back to how smoothly everything went. Far from being ogres out to grind my bones for bread, each person I spoke with was cordial and respectful, if not outright friendly. They were as eager to work out a realistic solution as I was – or *we* were, rather. I came away from the exercise with a clearly defined roadmap that paid off one debt and then another until, within just a very few months, all my debt was gone. In the process, I also came away with a new understanding of how some power that I cannot see or feel gives me the practical ability to do amazing things in my life – if I am willing to take action. And to have a little faith.

Since I learned to ride a bicycle myself as a child of maybe six or seven, I've never really wondered if I had lost the skill – even if I've gone a couple of years without hopping on a two-wheeler. We often hear the old saying that *it's like riding a bicycle – just hop back on and you'll remember.* And faith is like that, to me. Once you know that it works, belief in the ultimate unexplainable force is a powerful asset that you keep – and use – for life.

And, like the little boy who lived across the street, I'm sure enjoying the ride.

Thirteen: For the Record

I remember sitting in a large conference room once during the early days of my career on a team dealing with some public relations calamity when a grizzled old vet down at the end of the table said, "If it doesn't end up in the newspaper, then it never happened – that's the public record." Again, he was grizzled and old, so what he said might have been very correct in older, grizzlier times. I'm not so sure that it would be true in our modern digital-media age with blogs and YouTube and so forth. But I think the point he was making was very right in a different sort of way. We do each leave a public record. We each leave behind a book of our lives, filled chapter-by-chapter with the events, people, loves, losses, triumphs and tragedies – in all, the sum total of who we were and what we contributed to the larger story of humankind. I like to think of my life in the context of a book; there are new characters entering and exiting all the time, new twists and subplots, new obstacles and resolutions, and all of the classic themes of literature. Most appealing to me is the notion that I have no clue how the story will end. Tomorrow will be another page, followed by another and another and so on until the closing words. My book's been pretty entertaining so far.

One of my favorite personal parlor games is to scan the daily obituaries in my local paper – the public record of those who have passed on. I do it not so much to see if there might be names I recognize – occasionally there are – but to double-check to be sure that I'm not listed myself. I joke with my family that each day I browse the obituaries and don't see my name and picture automatically goes down in the plus column. But on top of that, I find it interesting to scan the photos and read the words to steal a glimpse into the lives of the dearly departed. Obituaries provide a *Reader's Digest* version of a person's book of life – *Cliff's Notes,* if you will.

You can glean much at first glance; the lengthier write-ups usually pay tribute to people who achieved great things in life – they built enterprises, contributed to charitable causes and generally left their mark scratched deeply on the landscape of the community. The youthful faces are nearly always associated with some disease or tragedy. Sadly, many – but not all – of the adolescent faces are linked to suicide, automobile accidents or drug overdose. My teenage son, who is a military history buff, can spot a World War II veteran in seconds; look closely and, sure enough, you find a mention of divisions and campaigns and commendations. A thousand of these vets die each day, many taking their often-untold stories with them.

Obituaries for older women are generally warm, wonderful and reassuring – many are devoted mothers and homemakers who leave legacies of family and dedication to neighborhoods, jobs and garden clubs. It was a privilege for me to write my mother's obituary and it was no stretch at all to come up with a lengthy list of good deeds and kind things to say. Women's obituaries reassure us that mothers are the glue that hold civilization together and, without them, our lives would be much more sterile and mathematical and cold. This is a personal choice, but I like to see obituary photos of the deceased from earlier years, when they were young and healthy and hearty. A man or woman may be eighty or ninety when they die, but I want to see what they looked like when they were twenty or thirty. That makes it easier for me to relate their lives to mine. It gives their lives – and mine – greater context.

When we write obituaries, creating the public record for a friend or loved one, we are forced to reduce an entire life down into just a few dozen words. So we look for talking points and sound bites. The first of which – coming right after name and dates of birth and death – usually deals with religion. Many write-ups go to great lengths to describe a person's steadfast and unwavering commitment to a faith or a congregation, often listing the number of decades at a certain parish, church jobs held, or terms served. And these write-ups are launched by often-imaginative statements that leave little doubt as to the subject's religious devotion:

John passed into the loving arms of his Savior...

Donna was called home to dwell in the house of her Lord...

Whether these persons were truly pious or not, these statements sometimes come across as last-chance pleas to ensure entrance into Heaven – religious letters of introduction, so to speak. They read like notes slipped along with a folded twenty-dollar bill to St. Peter at the Pearly Gates even as the newly departed stands in the queue, a final parting shout-out to readers in both Heaven and on Earth that this person did actually live a good and decent life. They serve as life insurance policies that we take out at the last minute to keep a loved one safe and protected as they board a plane or a ship and embark on a strange new journey to some unknown destination.

What we say about people in obituaries is indeed important. But it's tough to condense the full weight of a person's life down to five or six or even ten column inches. Sometimes the very best obituaries are simple and straightforward enough to call it like it is, shooting from the hip to say something simple like *He gave it his best shot... he was human and imperfect, and therefore prone to both successes and failures... he will be sorely missed.* Robert Louis Stevenson took the liberty of writing his own obituary in the form of the poem *Requiem* – one of my very favorite pieces of classic literature:

> *Under the wide and starry sky*
> *Dig the grave and let me lie*
> *Glad did I live and gladly die*
> *And I laid me down with a will.*
>
> *These be the words you grave for me:*
> *Here he lies where he longed to be*
> *Home is the sailor, home from the sea*
> *The hunter, home from the hill.*

There is something very honest and comforting in these words, an acceptance that life is an adventure and, by definition, a learning and growing experience. In our wanderings, we cross many seas and struggle across many hills. But in the end, we embrace the imperfect beauty of the world and surrender ourselves – hopefully with gladness – to the earth from which we came. I think that is the measure of a life well lived. We come, we do our best to leave fewer messes than we create, we add positive experiences to our brothers and sisters in life, we accept ourselves and others as we are, we strive to be close to the power that made us. We live, we learn, we die – with humility and gratitude.

These days, I see more and more obituaries – expanded features, usually – about young men and women who have fallen in combat overseas. I read these, knowing that somewhere on the other end of the story a family like mine has received a knock at the door and is just beginning the long and painful struggle for answers. Almost universally, stories of fallen soldiers contain a quote from a bereaved parent who cites devotion to freedom and country or other patriotic themes – almost as if reading from a prepared script. Parents of fallen soldiers have to say these things, for it gives them a reason – a noble something to grab onto – through which they can begin to look for some satisfactory justification. These deaths need purpose. And no parent wants to admit that they lost such a gigantic part of their lives and future for an unworthy cause.

So obituaries are really coping mechanisms of sorts – ways for us to resolve memories of the departed and create some form of closure. We can look at a printed story and read it and clip it out to save, and in doing so, gain some sense of physical finality. But there are other records, often unwritten, left behind for family and friends that aren't usually so black and white.

Like many who lose a close friend or relative, I went through a period of intense dreaming in the first year or two following Kerry's accident. My dreams were typically much the same, with a few minor variations. From the day that I first read the inch-thick official military accident report – complete with engineering studies, reconstructions and comments from senior officers and aviators who were infinitely familiar with both the pilot and his aircraft – I had committed every detail of his ninety-second flight to memory. In my dream, Kerry and I were together in the cockpit, merged as one. He was the wingman in a two-plane formation, so there was a constant need to pay attention to distance, angle of attack, speed and rate of climb. The gear came up, as did the flaps that make up the entire rear half of the jet's large wing. Then, with the simple push of a lever next to the throttle on the cramped left side of the cockpit, the plane's four jet nozzles rotated straight aft, turning the A/V8-B Harrier into a deadly forward-flying high-speed Marine ground-attack hotrod. That's what should have happened, anyway.

But the Harrier, notoriously billed as the military's most dangerous and unforgiving aircraft by far, is prone to failures. And a catastrophic failure is exactly what happened next. The massive flaps failed to retract into their normal flush position, streamlined for the natural laminar flow of air across the wing. Locked into the down position by a computer circuit board that had shorted out in the humid North Carolina air, the failed flaps instantly deflected thirty thousand pounds of thrust from the giant jet engine directly down and to the rear of the aircraft. In a split second, what the investigators called "flap impingement" violently tossed the aircraft into a vertical position, with its tail straight up and its nose pointing directly down toward the ground several hundred feet below. The powerful thrust of the jet nozzles, now blasting out horizontally, sent the doomed craft skidding off into the distance toward a slow but inevitable meeting with Mother Earth.

All pilots know there is a moment, usually during take-off or landing, when it is simply impossible to recover an aircraft – any aircraft – from a catastrophic malfunction. Salvation requires either speed or altitude or a combination of both. Kerry had neither. And so, as his wingman looked on and the two pilots shouted instructions and emergency procedures back and forth, the crippled plane did it's nose-down dance of death off to the south, over a low rise, and finally through a tall stand of pine trees and into the ground. At the last moment, there was an attempt to fire the rocket-powered ejection seat, but the craft was well outside the escape envelope. It was a futile gesture anyway – the chair malfunctioned, too.

It was over in an instant each time. In the dream, I was Kerry, and he was me, and we were together as one as we struggled to process way too many inputs – pilots call it overload – and ultimately lost the fight. There was a separation between us, though: I would wake up, and he wouldn't. But one night, I had a much different dream. We were walking – he and I – like giants in a land of little people. The world was quiet and colorful as we walked along a coastline, stepping gently over hills and homes, navigating our way through a graveyard that looked to we two Gullivers like row upon row of tiny dominoes. The sun was bright and it was a beautiful day and there was a great sense of calm and peace.

Then we were at a room at a hospital on the airbase – Kerry had led me there but left me outside the door as he entered. When I went inside, I found another man – an orderly, I think – folding my brother's clothes. He looked at me with a pleasant, easy smile and explained to me that Kerry was gone. He assured me that everything was okay and that I needn't worry – ever again – about my brother's fate. The man seemed both aware and unconcerned that a transition had occurred from this life and on into the next – he was purely matter-of-fact. His smile was comforting and gentle and reassuring.

I woke up breathing normally and deeply – not drenched in the usual cold sweat. I felt rested and peaceful. I lay in bed and pondered the meaning of the dream and worked to commit every detail to memory. It soothed me. I somehow knew it would be the last dream I ever had – or would need to have – about Kerry's death. I was now ready to move on. I have talked with many others who have had similar dreams following the tragic death of a loved one. I believe it is a natural part of the grieving process. Maybe these dreams are God's gifts to us. In the cockpit with Kerry, during those final few seconds, I came to the firm conclusion – I felt without doubt in my heart – that there comes a point in the process of death when we accept the inevitable and are blessed with an overwhelming sense of peace and serenity. A door opens, and we enter. We are welcomed into the great beyond. And I know there is no reason for fear.

I have a large manila envelope full of my brother's obituaries. Along with letters and cards, they came at me from everywhere in the weeks following the funeral. But perhaps the most significant written record of his life – or his death, anyway – came a full fourteen years after the accident that killed him.

In the summer of 2002, I packed up my family and bounded off to a small island tucked away along the world's second longest barrier reef off the coast of Belize. It was a rugged and remote place, with no paved roads and no cars, but also one of the most beautiful places I have ever seen. We lived in a big red shack twenty yards from the crystal-clear water and went shoeless for weeks on end. The community of about five hundred was poor by most standards, but the people were charming, marvelous and happy. We had no TV, so we read books and played cards in the evenings. We became very good at using our one-burner propane stove to make delicious meals from whatever we could scrounge, including fresh fish and lobster that we bought from the locals each afternoon. We opened up the big wooden flaps that covered the windows and let the Caribbean trade winds wash the freshness of thousands of miles of open ocean over us each day and night.

I was able to do my work in the mornings, rising early to enjoy fresh coffee and a sunrise on our breezy porch before strolling to the island's sand-floored Internet café to send and receive the day's assignments. I worked in the mornings, and then we all spent the afternoons sailing little skiffs in the breezy lagoon between our shore and the reef a mile or so out, or swimming at the "split" that cut the island in two.

One day while we were there, I received a strange email asking if I was the brother of a deceased Marine aviator named Kerry Dale. Out of curiosity, I replied. Thus began several months of contact with writers from the *Los Angeles Times* who were working on a series of feature stories on the failings of the Marines' beloved Harrier. I hadn't followed the news of the Harrier community for many years – life had marched on for me and my family – and I was surprised to learn that, in addition to my brother, forty-four other pilots had perished in the troubled aircraft. I was equally astonished to hear that more than a full third of the small Harrier fleet had been lost to accidents. The writers wanted to know if I was willing to participate in the story – apparently some families had opted not to. I eagerly agreed and sent them all the information I had once I returned to the United States. I met with one of the writers when he traveled through Dallas. I provided a quote or two along with photos and logbooks.

The four-part series rolled out just before Christmas of 2002, a year and three months after my mother passed away. Had the project surfaced while she was still alive, I doubt she would have had the strength to live through everything all over again, despite the tenacity that marked her life. There was still too much pain, too much rawness for her. But as with most things in God's world, events happen how and when they are supposed to, and I was ready and able to help – along with many others, including my father and sister, who gave the writers an inside peek at the losses shared by our collective families. The series of stories – which ended with individual profiles of each of the pilots – led to hearings in Congress on a subject that the Marine Corps continues to work very hard to squelch, and went on to win a Pulitzer Prize for The *Los Angeles Times* and its writers. I did my part for a brother and mother who couldn't. And, by telling a story that needed to be told, the series helped to broaden the public record for a great group of fine young men who were needlessly lost.

But a great many other stories never make it to the front page, even though they should. It's almost cliché to say that the very best records we can leave are in the form of what others say after we are gone.

I worked for a man once who was all business in both his conduct and his demeanor. He was friendly and sociable, to be sure. But in matters of commerce and daily life around the office, he could be a bit aloof and cold at times. He was a good man – a loving husband and father – and certainly fair to those of us who worked for him. In a business where any copywriter is only as good as the last ad written, this man stood by me at a time in my life when I needed a backstop, and for that I am grateful. But he was, at midlife, focused – as many business owners are – on clients and billings and forecasts and profits. In short, he was a bottom-line sort of guy.

Over the years that I worked for the firm, there were a number of acquisitions and mergers, culminating with the sale of the entire shop to a major multinational advertising agency. When the dust settled from this final transition, we found ourselves with lots of new faces around the office. One, in particular, was a veteran warhorse who had been around the industry for decades in Dallas – well known by many at all echelons of the advertising community. His integration into the agency had been awkward – mergers have a tendency to wreak havoc on hierarchies – and there was a natural tension between he and the established managers, including my boss, who shared with me on more than one occasion that he didn't "know what to do with him." There were politics involved. And egos.

One day not too long after coming aboard, this new man dropped dead from a heart attack. It happened suddenly, literally overnight, and caught everyone quite off guard. Naturally, all of the senior managers attended the funeral. I did not attend, but my boss did – and returned a changed man. Apparently the funeral had brought together thousands of people – friends and well-wishers from all walks of life and all social strata. Not only important business people, but also neighbors and everyday acquaintances – the gardener, the dry cleaner, the grocery store cashier – who all remembered him with equal admiration. This man had obviously affected a great many people during his humble spin on the planet. His eulogy focused not on his many accomplishments – these were commonly known – but on the myriad small things he had done in his life to leave a positive impact in the community and make the world a better place. It was obvious to all that he was no ordinary person, and the measure of his life had gone far beyond the basic goals we all aspire to – financial security, a good loving family, a solid reputation – to create a truly lasting legacy. Chief among the man's attributes was a genuine gift of humility; none of us who had known him so briefly around the office had any idea of the many things he had done – large and small – to *walk the walk* in God's world.

This man at my office who passed from us so suddenly, while never amassing a huge financial empire, had clearly built great personal wealth – the kind that mattered. Ironically, my boss, who was earning money hand over fist, seemed locked into a carnal fight for survival of sorts – striving to be seen as a winning hunter/gatherer, just like our ancient cave-dwelling forebears. But the funeral had impacted him greatly, and he visited my office upon returning to say over and over again that *that was the way to live a life,* and *that was the way to be measured upon our departure.* I saw changes in him from then on until I left the company – subtle shifts, but changes nonetheless. We all learn from the examples and inspirations of others as we grow older – some at younger stages than others – and we all have the chance to change our objectives to be more in tune with the guiding directions of God's will for us.

So I have come to believe from my study of our collective human record that we are what make God work in this life. Our actions – singularly and collectively – create God and show His presence. We are the tools that bring God to life, writing a divine record through the ways we treat others and ourselves each day. Instead of searching for a God that works, we have the power to simply create one – by doing those things that demonstrate the principles of God to our families, our friends, our neighbors and to the world at large. Our efforts can lead to a heaven in the here-and-now. In a sense, we become the face of God to everyone around us – dishing out compassion, care, love and good works to all in need. I have heard it said that our personal ethics aren't defined by what we do in public – what is seen or known about us in the news or in our obituaries – but by what we do when we are alone – by ourselves and with God. Our ethics and legacies are shaped by our contributions to God's collective record.

Some religions believe that we will stand before God in judgment upon our death, and that He will review our accomplishments as recorded in the *Book of Life.* But the book of our lives is what we write here now. So it is how our record is reviewed in the here-and-now that really matters.

In my book, that's fit for print.

Fourteen: The Captain and Me

I have many spiritual guides. I use the word "guides" because I think the word "teachers" is misleading in this context. As I stated earlier in the book, I don't believe that anyone truly knows any more about the true nature of spirituality than the rest of us. But I do think that we are all guides for each other; we can freely share our lessons along the spiritual path and learn from the experiences of others. In fact, I think this approach is infinitely stronger than simply relying on the teaching – no matter how divinely inspired – of any single individual. The inputs of many are exponentially greater than the input of one, and also considerably less dangerous. We use our God-given reasoning abilities to synthesize things we learn from many different quarters to create an understanding of spirituality – of God – that works for us.

I have one spiritual guide who I have asked on numerous occasions to share with me what he has learned on his path to God. Each time, he answers by telling me he'll let me know once he's begun the journey. I love that answer. What he is saying, of course, is that the farther he believes himself to be down the spiritual path that we all must follow, the farther he is aware that his travels will take him. In essence, he is saying that putting one foot on the spiritual path only shows how immense and long and winding the journey can be.

Instead of finding that daunting, I find it extremely exhilarating. I like the idea that there is so much more to learn, that I will get to spend the rest of my days here on Earth going from the infancy that I find myself in today into some semblance of childhood and then on to adolescence and eventually adulthood as a spiritual being. And then maybe I get to start all over again in infancy. Because I will know at that point, further still, how long and winding the road can be. To me that is wondrous and awesome. The good news – the *great* news – is that the journey never ends, at least for me. Some are satisfied to stay where they are, *right here and right now,* and that's fine for them. They are not seekers. Or, maybe they are but they find fear and uncertainty in forging ahead on the journey. There is a certain amount of comfort in remaining in the known world. As sailors of old said as they pointed off to the distant horizon, *"Out there be monsters."*

I've heard it said that we are not humans on a spiritual journey, but rather spiritual beings on a human journey. I like that. I truly do believe that the essence of my life – my spiritual core – may have existed prior to this life and will certainly exist again, in some form, after this life ends. All faiths have that as a goal of sorts. Some think of the afterlife as the end, and all of our worldly endeavors here on Earth are simply the means to that end. The primary quest of all the monotheistic faiths is, after all, to get to Heaven. I find that view disturbing and depressing. It's saddening to think that what I'm living today isn't the real thing, but rather a run-up to the Big Show. That makes it too easy for me to lose sight of the importance and relevance and meaning of the Heaven I can choose to create around myself in the here-and-now. *This* is what's real.

I certainly do believe in the idea of an afterlife – but I'm also convinced that none of us has a real clue what it will be. The poor man who died behind the dumpster back in Chapter Six knows, but none of us alive today has the faintest idea. The Bible talks about cities with streets paved with gold and endless wedding feasts, and the Koran apparently promised the 9/11 hijackers a sizeable number of virgins, but those are earthly manifestations – projections of what we know and understand as humans into a realm that we know nothing about. Heaven is, by definition, not Earthly. I think it's interesting that most religious folks roll their eyes at the mere mention of reincarnation. But isn't that what the idea of Heaven is all about? Isn't that what being *born again* means?

I am firmly ensconced in middle age – darned close to fifty as of this writing. But I look back to when I was just out of college and how smart I thought I was about virtually everything. If you had a question, I could come up with an answer – any subject, any time, to any degree. I prided myself on my ability to act intelligently in conversation about any topic – politics, the arts, relationships, you name it. And I don't think I am unique in that – I see the same attitude in my oldest child who has now reached young adulthood. And I see it in scads of other wet-behind-the-ears Gen-Xers I encounter out in the workplace. Maybe this stems from the notion we all get through high school and college that, when we reach adulthood, we're supposed to have a pretty solid grip on most everything.

When I got into recovery from alcohol and drug abuse at age thirty, I learned that finding out about myself and working to find a new spiritual path in my life involved removing all vestiges of self-pride from my being. I had to start with a blank sheet of paper and work from there. As the saying goes: I had to learn to be a "part of" and not "apart from" – which means that I had to learn humility and open-mindedness. Simply put, I needed a bit of ego-deflation. I had to learn that if I shut my mouth and opened my ears there was still an amazing amount in this world for me to know. In short, I had to learn that everything that I thought I already knew was working more against me than for me. I had to learn to be re-teachable. I had to admit that I knew nothing.

I think back to perhaps the most intensive learning experience I've ever had – the summer I joined the Merchant Marine. And to my teacher: the weathered captain of my first deep-sea tug.

I nearly died my first day aboard the *Mister Randy*. Within twenty-four hours, I had traveled from the quiet comfort of the Houston suburbs to the rolling swells of offshore Louisiana, traveling by van overnight through Cameron and Intracoastal City, and then by sleek-but-bumpy crew boat south through the muddy brown outflow of the Mississippi River and into the deep blue water of the Gulf of Mexico and finally to the slippery decks of my new home. Beyond geography, I had leapt a great cultural divide, as well. I was a college boy, tossed in among men who had largely not seen high school – a rugged Cajun bunch with a language and diet all their own and a curious eye toward obvious outsiders like me.

After a sleepless first night rolling side to side in my bunk – I would learn later the trick of stuffing blankets and life preservers under the outside edge of the mattress to wedge myself against the bulkhead – I was handed a long metal boathook – a *gaff* – and thrust out onto the rolling wet stern deck of the tug to go right to work "running anchors." I had a partner – a large bandana-wearing curly haired man whose only name appeared to be "Biggun" – but he had not yet stopped looking at me sideways, through slit eyes, enough to explain to me what running anchors entailed. These were the Wild West days of oilfield work in the Gulf of Mexico, the domain of men who fled the cities back east in search of gold in the hills – mountain men and roughriders with a survival code based purely on Darwinism; only the strong would survive. OSHA had not yet been invited into this brave new world. Training was non-existent, and injuries were common; I was to see half a dozen fellow deckhands leave the boat over my many months with broken feet, twisted arms, puncture wounds or worse.

The *Mister Randy* and one other vessel were tasked with supporting a large pipe-laying barge that was building, one forty-foot segment at a time, an undersea artery through the gulf that would bring crude oil from the vast network of offshore platforms to refineries on shore. As workmen on the barge welded pipe segments together, the huge craft inched itself forward by winching in the anchors that strung far off its bows and letting out on the anchors that led from its stern. Each anchor weighed roughly four tons and was secured to the barge – two to each corner – by a mile or more of heavy cable. In addition to this, each anchor also had a smaller wire rope that led straight up to the surface, attached to a round, white metal buoy perhaps ten feet in diameter. Our job aboard the tug was to snag these big buoys, reel up the anchor using one of the huge winches built onto the stern deck of the tug, and run it a mile out ahead of the barge and drop it so that the entire process could march forth. It was round-the-clock work – always wet and dangerous – that involved intricate choreography between the two deckhands slipping about on the always-awash deck below, and the captain who sat in a caged-in "doghouse" on the deck above and operated the winch while at the same time driving the ship.

As we came up on each anchor buoy that morning, bringing them banging down the port side of the tug, I eagerly leaned out with my gaff to snare the connecting cable that would connect to our winch, which would then drag up the four-ton anchor. I was completely unaware that each time I did this, I was putting myself between the gunwale of the vessel and the heavy steel cable, which would, if we were to somehow let go of the heavy anchor, pin me in a snap and cut me in half like scissors in the blink of an eye. I only learned of this later, wolfing down lunch in the galley, as the captain pointed out my death-defying ignorance from his private table across the room. He said it all matter-of-factly, without looking up from his meal. I looked over to Biggun, who remained buried silently in a bowl of gumbo.

Over time, I would see the simple chain of events that could have instantly caused my death occur many times. The slip of a hand on the winch control, a frayed cable snapping suddenly, a missed connection in rough seas between the buoy and the winch cable. Each time I saw this, I witnessed my own death. Following the immutable laws of physics, the weight of the anchor would pull down on the cable, slicing me neatly in two with cleaver-like precision. And there were half-a-dozen other situations where I found myself in imminent danger only afterwards; survival offshore clearly favored the fittest – or the most ignorant.

Within the first few days, I learned a great deal about how little I knew of the real world – not only about machinery and engineering and working in dangerous situations at sea, but also about people. The captain wasted no opportunity to point out my ignorance.

A dozen years later when I entered sobriety, I was once again introduced to the concept. I was told that, in order to become teachable and to learn what I needed to know to stay sober, I had to first be willing to admit that I knew nothing. In a very real way, I had to learn to use the words "I don't know." At first, they were unfamiliar words to me, and I was hesitant to use them. In my professional field, I believed that I was valued based on what I knew, not what I didn't know, and I had always made it a point to let everyone know exactly how much I knew about every little thing. If I didn't actually know something, I was darned good at making everyone believe that I did. So it was quite revolutionary for me to one day begin introducing the simple words "I don't know" into my lexicon.

Marvelously, I learned that my world did not end. I was never excused from a meeting or shown the door to carry away my ignorance in shame. I learned to follow up the phrase with the words "... but I can go and find out." And, when I did that, I found that daily life started to work much more smoothly. I felt much more at ease in my interactions with others. I felt much more plugged in and, dare I say, humble. This became a stepping stone to learning that it's perfectly okay to say that we don't really have a clue about the broad nature of spirituality or God or the Great Beyond. It's okay to admit that we want to go and find out. This can become the starting place for incredible growth and learning. In fact, it can be key to our spiritual survival.

One of the great benefits that come with this view of spirituality as a living, breathing journey that never ends is that we get to acknowledge the fact that we are always *exactly where we are supposed to be* at any given point on the journey. What I understood about God prior to my brother's death in 1988 – when I really needed a God that would work in my life – was exactly what I was supposed to know at that point. I knew either a great deal or very little, depending on how I look back at that time. But it's unarguable that I knew precisely what I needed to know in order to begin the quest that has brought me to where I am today. The corollary to this is that ten years from now, I will likely have a completely different level of understanding than what I have today. I will no doubt have the experiences and insights to take a look back at what I've written here and either toss the whole work in the trash or perhaps add a sequel. Who knows?

Along with this amazing idea that we all know exactly what we are supposed to know at any given time in our lives is the equally magnificent notion that we are always doing the best job we are able to do with ourselves at that moment. We make decisions – good, bad or otherwise – based on what we know, what we feel, what we understand, and what our needs and desires are at a precise moment in our life. We may look back with regret at some of the things we have done – I know that I am certainly able to do that – but we must also understand that we have always done the very best with the mental and spiritual tools at our disposal. We should never really have guilt in our lives. The relief that we are provided by this is immeasurable. We are able to forgive ourselves for our shortcomings much more easily. Instead of loading ourselves with shame that can continue to drag us down and cause still more poor behaviors, we can learn from what we have done – both good and bad – and work to make our lives better and more fulfilling for ourselves and the world around us.

There are many who say that God has stopped speaking to us. They speak of the Bible as a complete document, totally without error – *inerrant* is the word most often used – in both meaning and context, perfect in every sense of the word. They believe that, even though the Bible was cobbled together over the course of many, many centuries by many thousands of human hands, and that many, many good books with scriptural relevance were eliminated from the commonly used versions of the Bible we have today, there is no room for updating or modifying the work in any way, shape or form. I find it discouraging that God did all of that talking in so many ways through so many people in so many places for so long, and then dried up on us. Interestingly, at about the time that God supposedly stopped speaking, we as humans started growing and learning. We took the naked facts of God's world and created frameworks around them through the sciences of mathematics and physics. We studied and explored – using the natural gifts for inquiry that God gave us – and created a newer, bigger and better platform for understanding the world around us. So why wouldn't God have come along with us for that ride?

I, for one, choose to believe that God – whatever God is – has certainly not stopped speaking. Instead, perhaps we have stopped listening. Or, worse yet, we are able to look the Creator squarely in the face and receive new messages through a dozen real-life channels every day – yet we ignore what we so freely hear and see. God could be shouting right at us, and we close our eyes and ears. We are unwilling or unable to admit that there is far more to learn – about spirituality, about religion, about God.

Over a period of many months aboard the *Mister Randy*, the captain and I developed an interesting and unique relationship. As the days passed, I grew from a naïve and innocent newbie – he called me "Pinkie" many times during the rough first few weeks and demanded to know who my father was, mistakenly thinking that I had arrived aboard his tiny ship purely by virtue of a relationship to some company executive – into a far more mature and savvy young adult. In short, the captain poked and prodded and pushed me up the "I don't know" learning curve at a breakneck pace.

As a matter of day-to-day survival, I learned to rip the sleeves from my fraternity T-shirts and wear them inside out. I grew a beard and perfected a salty new language. I learned to drink the near-toxic raisin-jack that the cook and engineer kept as a brain cell-killing living culture in a five-gallon bucket hidden behind one of the massive diesels in the engine room. I bonded with Biggun, so that he and I formed a near-perfect union – my slightly more polished sophistication merging seamlessly with his rougher, more brutish but far simpler demeanor. We became a good team and learned to watch out for each other. We would go through tempests and trials, hurricanes and calamities together on the high seas, and watch many others come and go through injury or firings or even desertion. Biggun became my friend.

But the captain, late at night up on the bridge and far out of earshot of others in the crew, would lower his walls and open himself up to me. He taught me much about the ways of boats and the seas – all I had to do was ask – and prove to him that I was teachable – I had to *want* to know. He showed me the basics of navigation – how to use Loran to triangulate radio signals so that we could plot our position at sea, far away from the coast. He explained latitude and longitude and how we could pinpoint our location on Earth to within a few yards. He showed me how to use right triangles to plot lines of course and bearing on the charts, a technique I use to this day while other sailors I know persist on using much less elegant parallel rulers. Each time I pull out my triangles aboard my own boat, I think of the captain and our nights alone on the bridge talking – teaching and learning – quietly under the dim light of the lamp at the chart table.

He never dropped his guard with me completely; a captain is God aboard any ship and must never appear to favor any one member of a crew over another. There was protocol to follow, even aboard a greasy tugboat in the middle of the Gulf oil patch. One morning, after I had scrubbed the entire length of the port side of the main deck – starting at the bow at sunrise with a push broom, box of washing powder and garden hose – I noticed a stream of yellow runoff mixing with my own pure water and sloshing out the scuppers near the stern. I looked up to see the captain standing on the bridge wing two decks above looking off into the distance and urinating. He could no more look down at me as he watered my clean deck than I could acknowledge the special place I think he had found in his quiet world for me. It was a sunny, breezy morning, and I'm sure he was smiling. He was the captain, and I was a deckhand, and that is the way it was. That's the way it was supposed to be.

By forcing me to acknowledge exactly how little I knew, the captain paved the way for me to learn. And then he willingly shared with me all the things that I sought to know – all I had to do was ask. Will I ever understand the full measure of everything I stand to learn from others I meet on my individual spiritual journey? Will I ever know everything there is to know about the God that drives my life?

I don't know.

Fifteen: Who Speaks for God?

I'm not a Trekkie, but I do enjoy watching *Star Trek* reruns. Mom and I had great fun watching the show in the evenings back in the seventies and made a game of figuring out how an episode fell into our pre-set categories of Plot A, B or C. Each of the eighty or so episodes falls generally into one of these plotlines, though characters and times and places change – as do the campy sets. In our categorization scheme, Plot A involved the crew of the Enterprise encountering some ethereal galactic being – a stellar cloud or invisible whatsit making its way through the universe to explore or wreak havoc or often both. Plot B involved encounters with classic foes like the Romulans or Klingons or other real-life, physical enemies. And Plot C always had the stalwart cast dealing with some Earth-like or human-created situation that was leading to the imminent destruction of something or someone or other. Regardless of plot, each script was further enriched by the inevitable story of unrequited love – a maiden or queen or damsel in distress rescued and left broken-hearted by Kirk, Spock or even McCoy. And, of course, there were those darned dilithium crystals that always gave Scotty such fits.

The reason these forty-year-old episodes are still so wildly popular and in a seemingly perpetual state of rerun is because they dealt with timeless and universal themes – the struggle for survival, love and loyalty, the hunger for learning and adventure, the quest for life's fulfillment, and also how and what we believe – all wrapped up inside the eternal battle between good and evil. Like modern-day Shakespeare, these episodes are morality plays. And even though they are acted out on cheesy stages in strange new worlds, the stories are as meaningful and relevant today as they were in the sixties – maybe even more so.

One episode that has always stuck out for me is titled *For the World is Hollow and I Have Touched the Sky*, which falls squarely into the category of Plot C. In the story, a civilization that has lived for ten thousand years on an asteroid is on a collision course with a densely populated planet. Unknown to its inhabitants, the asteroid is actually a space ship built by their ancestors to carry them away from a failing world and toward a new paradise. The ship is under the control of an ancient Oracle, a device that contains all knowledge and wields all power. The asteroid's inhabitants worship the Oracle and follow its guidance completely. The Oracle – through its "book of knowledge" – tells them everything and provides all answers. And they adhere to it rigidly and blindly – under penalty of death – even though, as Kirk and crew know, its original data is obviously out of sync with present real-world conditions.

Hmmm. This sounds strangely familiar.

On Spaceship Earth, we have our own versions of the Oracle and also our own various sacred books of knowledge.

Of course the Oracle is a metaphor for religion, for they are both given our awe and worship as instruments that alone understand humankind's true purpose and destiny. We believe in them and follow them simply because we always have – the many generations who have come before assure us that this is where all answers are to be found. And we also unfailingly trust in the answers contained within our various books of knowledge. We hold them aloft and revere them and give them tremendous powers, consciously ignoring whether we know them to be right or wrong.

I read a startling study recently that presented the results of a religious quiz given to thousands of avowed evangelicals. More than half couldn't cite five of the Ten Commandments, and an alarming number believed that Sodom and Gomorrah were married. About ten percent believed that Joan of Arc was Noah's wife. And our knowledge of world religions is even worse; nearly one in five defined Ramadan as the Jewish Day of Atonement. This is because many – if not most – people who claim that the Bible is the infallible and complete word of God have never actually read most of it or studied the broader subject of religion in any great detail. Instead, they simply buy into the aura and mystique that surrounds it all. *If so many people say it's the answer, then it simply must be.* Few have the courage to question the Oracle.

One of the interesting things about discussing religion or, more specifically, raising questions about traditional religious thinking, is that nearly everyone comes at the topic from a different level of understanding – a different starting spot along the seeker spectrum. As I've developed my topics for this book, I've largely avoided letting too many others around me know the specifics of my work – they know that I'm writing a book about living and searching out different ways to look at religion and spirituality. It's not that I avoid discussing these issues with anyone; it's just that any time the subject comes up, we tend to start with the same initial set of comments and questions.

The moment most people realize that we are discussing in-depth questions about age-old ways of believing in God, they give a glancing look side to side – as if checking to be sure that no one will overhear the conversation – and then go on to say they've always had those questions but maybe just assumed that they were the only ones who were out-of-sync with the religious world around them. Indeed, my experience has been that virtually everyone I have spoken with about this subject has welcomed the topic as long overdue. More than a few have voiced the tragic view that, while they've always questioned some basic ideas of religion, they could never be seen in their neighborhoods and social circles as someone who didn't toe the line or play an active part in the local community church. I think this is sad – but also perfectly understandable. It shows the strength of conformity and of tradition; few are willing to be the ones to rock the boat or serve as the grain of sand in the oyster.

Once the door to discussion is cracked, most conversations begin with an initial set of simple questions or comments. These are the elemental thoughts that first arise within persons who have taken baby steps outside the comfortable boundaries of faith.

Isn't the Bible merely a bunch of historical stories? Was Jesus a God or just a really good teacher? How was Mary a virgin? Was there really a Noah's Ark? Were miracles real? Can babies sin? Will I see my dog in Heaven?

These are certainly all good questions that show a desire to dangerously search for answers outside of the known, but they are also only prerequisites for truly stepping across the line and jumping headfirst into the kind of open-ended, open-minded learning that not only opens up entirely new fields of religious and spiritual study, but could also serve to provide new relevance and confirmation to existing beliefs.

They are the fundamentals; in my experience, these types of questions form the basis of the class we might call Seekers 101.

And that's because these questions only begin to scratch the surface of evaluating the real meaning, history and role of religion in our spiritual lives. They are a step in the right direction, but they are only a step – one that should be followed surely and positively with a march to true inquiry. To ask these questions, and focus solely on this level of query, is to ponder the nature of the bark on certain trees when it is the entire forest that must be viewed critically – from way up high overhead.

My biggest question about the Christian faith has never been brought up at the Seeker 101 level, or even by any of the religious experts whose books I have studied. In fact, I've never seen it addressed at all. My question deals with the whole premise behind the sacrifice that Jesus allegedly made for mankind upon the cross of Calvary. And that is: who required this sacrifice? And why was a sacrifice required? And finally – the really big part – how exactly does this sacrifice dissolve away my alleged sins?

Having spent a fair bit of time poring through the Old Testament, I see many references made to animal sacrifices. These were commonplace in the ancient Hebrew world – all of history, really – and are described in intricate detail in the opening verses of the book of Leviticus. In these age-old rites, and for reasons not fully understood by me, the ritual sacrifice of a living being – quite often a lamb – had the mystical power to help us clean our slate with the Creator. We could put our failings into the body of an animal and by spilling its blood send those shortcomings off into oblivion. In the book of Genesis, Abraham was given the opportunity to sacrifice a ram in the place of his son Isaac – so animals could obviously serve as proxies for humans. Or maybe a slaughtered animal, charred with fire to deliver a "sweet smell," acted simply as a gift to God. Call that a heavenly barbeque. Whatever the reason, there existed in ancient times some strange notion that the killing of some living being – usually on an altar and nearly always involving the celebratory spilling of blood – would appease God and help us to improve our standing in His eyes. We find this same practical belief in the traditions of the ancient Egyptians and the Aztecs of Central America, as well as among primitive tribes still hidden away in the remote jungles of Borneo.

Somewhere along the way in the tradition of sacrifice, ancient priests realized that if lambs or other small, helpless animals did an okay job of pleasing our otherworldly master, then a human sacrifice would surely up the ante. And while we might raise our eyebrows at cannibalistic and barbaric tribes that practice human sacrifice in far-off corners of the world – calling them heathens or savages – we seem to accept this as a noble and sacred concept when it comes to the "full perfect and human sacrifice" that Jesus made of himself upon the cross. Jesus is referred to as the "lamb of God" numerous times in Christian liturgy. And so Jesus merely carried forth the tradition of the ritualistic sacrifice of living beings set forth early in the Old Testament, even down to the spilling of His blood at the tip of a spear wielded by a Roman soldier at the foot of the cross. To this day, we pour His figurative blood at the altar and relish its amazing power to wash away our many sins.

But this implies that there is some power somewhere who would demand this kind of sacrifice of us – or, more personally, demand it of Jesus. You can't make a payment for something unless there is a commercial partner on the other end of the transaction who is writing out the bill and expecting a remittance. Is God the one who demands this payment? Is it God who sets the price of our freedom from a state of sin as a human life? As with the story of Abraham and Isaac, does God have some fascination with the idea of fathers sacrificing their own sons to – quite ironically – find favor with God or prove one's faith or make the world a better place? No doubt there are complicated and intricate theological answers to these questions; biblical apologists have come up with answers to everything – some so ludicrous that they simply boggle the mind. But, to me, this is an issue that absolutely must be addressed. And, indeed, it would need to be answered to my complete satisfaction before I could in any way throw myself down upon the ground in thankful and blind praise to Jesus for giving His life as a sacrifice upon the cross to pay for my very human shortcomings.

In actuality, much of the liturgy and tradition of the Christian faith – and many other contemporary faiths, as well – comes to us as holdovers from earlier legends and belief systems that stretch back to the dawn of man. A story like the one of infant Moses floating in a basket down the river can be found in Babylonian lore that extends back a thousand years before the ancient Hebrews. And there are numerous other examples to be explored – and a host of other books that would do a far better job of explaining them than I could dare to do here.

But the point is, there is vast empirical proof available to the thinking and inquisitive mind to show that nearly all of what we see, hear and accept as hard truth in modern religion is allegorical and figurative in nature. There is fact and there is fiction in our world. And there also is no problem – and no condemnation in God's eyes, I believe – with us doing our part as children of God and important elements of this amazing world to get a realistic grip on which is which.

A standard religious comeback to all question-asking is the all-powerful trump card of *faith*. Instead of pondering these things, you simply must have *faith*. Remember, the Oracle knows all. The "you must have faith" response to me comes across much like a mother's *because I told you so.*

It's a pat answer to everything. End of thought, end of discussion, end of inquiry.

As for the elemental questions my friends may ask, I do my best to avoid answering them. I don't know the answers, and it's not for me to speculate. I know what works for me, but I wouldn't presume to know what might work best for others. Many religious authorities say that they have the answers – and might call my faith into question for suggesting that they do not – but I believe that truly nobody knows. Every theory can be called a science, and every science can be called a theory. All we can know is what our eyes and ears and minds and study of the facts that surround us might suggest. And this means we are entitled to peer a little bit sideways at the Oracle.

Back to the point about sin. From the earliest time I can remember, I've had a concern with the general notion that I am a sinner. Do I do bad things? Are there gaps in my life that would keep me distanced from the way that my Creator – whatever that is – wants me to live this life in a way that delivers total fulfillment and serves my fellow traveler? Of course, yes. I am a human being, blessed with intelligence and the faculties to think and act in relation to the world around me – people, circumstances and things – and in the process of learning and growing I will always make mistakes. Some of these are innocent and others are not. But I think that a defining characteristic of humanity is that we all possess both good and bad traits. Our self-will and curiosity are the engines that drive the human story. While each of us is at a different point on the good/bad continuum, none of us is firmly planted exactly at either end of the scale. Despite the overwhelming selfless good she did in her life, Mother Teresa undoubtedly did things – including broadly questioning the very existence of God – that cast her as sinful to at least someone. And even Hitler loved his dog.

Everything about contemporary western religion hinges on the premise that we are inherently bad creatures and must find some way to pay for our sins and become good again – redeemed – in God's eyes. *We must be saved.* As individuals, we didn't even do anything to earn this original burden – Eve supposedly brought all that on in the Garden of Eden, all for her want of a good Granny Smith. Yet, this concept of the upward move from sin toward perfection and salvation is the very foundation upon which the Judeo-Christian world is built. From the moment that Eve collapsed into her craving in the early verses of Genesis – in one of two versions of creation contained in that book – we have been continually on the defensive with God. We have been sent to the corner as misbehaving children – something that to me seems just a wee bit unfair. I'm not saying that the concept of original sin is wrong – it may well be right – but I am suggesting that it's one of those subjects that need to be examined, and checked out pretty closely, if we are to have a realistic working concept of how God might work. Wouldn't we rather think of ourselves as inherently good and perfect, made in the very image of the God who created us? I know I would.

I guess I'm just one who has questioned the idea of the Oracle from the very beginning. I know that the voices that have spoken for God over the millennia are human, and therefore open targets to intense questioning and doubt. These voices have often spoken in a language that goes against everything I believe about my unique relationship with a loving God. Here is a prayer from the Episcopal Communion service that I'm sure I said a thousand times before ever actually paying attention to the words. It's called the Prayer of Humble Access.

> *We do not presume to come to this thy Table, O merciful Lord, trusting in our own righteousness, but in thy manifold and great mercies. We are not worthy so much as to gather up the crumbs under thy Table. But thou art the same Lord, whose property is always to have mercy: Grant us therefore, gracious*

Lord, so to eat the flesh of thy dear Son Jesus Christ, and to drink his blood, that our sinful bodies may be made clean by his body, and our souls washed through his most precious blood, and that we may evermore dwell in him, and he in us. Amen.

Apart from the blood imagery and an oblique plea for mercy – which gives me still more cause for question – the part about this that causes the most concern is the statement that *we are not worthy so much as to gather up the crumbs under thy Table.* Where did this come from? This, along with most of the other liturgy of the early Episcopal Church, was written during the earliest days of Anglicanism by Thomas Cranmer. Were he alive today, I would love to have a cup of coffee with him, to perhaps glean insights into why we – God's marvelous creations – should make such a groveling and sniveling admission. Who would want to join in a relationship with a Creator who would be our guide, our source of love and compassion, and our anchor to the living world as if we were dogs who did not deserve the opportunity to scrounge around for table scraps? (To be fair, this prayer was removed from Episcopal liturgy when the denomination moved from Rite I to Rite II some forty years ago – but it still pops up regularly during worship services at many older and more traditional churches.)

One thing I do very much like about an Episcopal worship service is the music – and that is a general statement that I also freely make about virtually every religious service I have attended in numerous flavors of multiple faiths. The music is definitely awesome – one of the best things organized religion has ever given us. There is something quite enchanting about the sounds of uplifted human voices echoing resoundingly throughout vaulted chambers. And nothing can create goose bumps or bring a tear to the eye like a full-bore, well-trained church choir, complete with carillon bells and a grand old pipe organ at a Christmas Eve Midnight Mass.

Outside of Handel's Messiah, one of the prettiest pieces any choir can sing in such a setting is the *Kyrie Eleison*. It's a simple three-line phrase of a larger plea that, in some of the longer and more harmonically developed versions, carries on for eternity, with lovely tenor and alto parts flowing beneath angelic and dainty sopranos and all built firmly on deep and resonant bass voices. To this day it is fun to sing. It goes simply:

Kyrie Eleison
Christe Eleison
Kyrie Eleison

Maybe because it is sung in the original Greek, I never paid much attention to it's content – *Lord have mercy, Christ have mercy, Lord have mercy.* To my mind, mercy is an action that we would normally request from someone or some institution that is about to cause us harm. In a practical sense, we ask for mercy when we are in imminent danger, moments away from being put to death by a conquering enemy. We ask a judge for leniency – a nice way of begging for mercy – when we have been found guilty and are about to be sentenced to a lengthy prison sentence. I believe that this idea that we need to continually beg for mercy from a benevolent creator who seems to have us constantly marked for retribution comes from the same place as our obsession with calling ourselves inherently sinful. Somewhere along the line, someone in the powerful corridors of religion landed on these negative ideas, and landed firmly. And so they wrote them solidly into our religious life. Sin and guilt – and the continual need to beg for mercy – have become the founding ideas behind faith and worship. They are cornerstones of our relationship with God. They are what give the Oracle and its magic book such grand and unfounded power.

In my personal quest for a true understanding of a God that works, I do not question whether these notions are right or wrong. But I do question whether or not we are to accept them blindly, *on faith.*

I would hope that every person who reads this comes away with a new and powerful understanding of the unique and personal relationship we each have with our Creator. We are free, encouraged and empowered to challenge our God and to grow by doing so. We are free to challenge what others have to say about the ways we should believe – for truly no one knows more than we are capable of learning for ourselves. We are free to question the tired old staples that we hear everyday in religion that are, in fact, subtle ploys designed to *prevent* us from questioning and draw us ever-deeper into age-old and stagnant ways of thinking. For example, tune into religious broadcasting, either on the radio or television, and within an hour at most you'll hear a booming-voiced preacher make a disparaging reference to the sad state of the world in which we live. You'll hear about the unchecked rise in vice and sin and corruption and how our moral values are at an all-time low and falling further still. You'll hear that the world is in its worst state in history, shot through with shallow facades and meaningless focus on false gods like money, pornography, lust and power. And you'll hear that these overwhelming negative forces are pushing us imminently over the edge and into the abyss. As Chicken Little would say, the sky is indeed falling.

Hmmm. Really?

I submit to you that, far from living in the Dark Days, we are living in the most positive, uplifting and generally progressive period in humankind's history, including, I would hope, a new Age of Enlightenment in religion that will occur over the coming decades. Certainly, there are problems the world over. We have crime and wars and corruption and deceit and all forms of other general debauchery. There is plenty of bad stuff to point at. But look around at how much good we see. Look at the way global communication has helped to foster growth and learning. See how a more transparent world has brought previously hidden vices out into the open. Yes, we see the many bad things, but maybe that's only because we are better able to see them. Yes, we see many terrible and deceitful acts being done in the name of organized religion – but we also see incredible works of charity and selfless giving. For every Ted Haggard, Jim Bakker or Osama bin Laden, there are many more Mother Teresas.

We must challenge these broad generalizations when we hear them. If not directly, then at least in our own minds. We should understand that the need to paint the world as bleak and dreary is an age-old technique used by church builders to rally the faithful together for the cause. You can't very well raise an army if you don't have an enemy. You can't solve a problem if you don't have one. You can't save the sinners unless they know how soul-less and doomed their lives really are.

In one of many conversations I had with my mother on the subject of why it is so important to affiliate my family with a local church congregation, she made the simple, bold and motherly assertion that *it is important that your children be raised in some sort of church family.* To her, that was the critical issue – that we follow the crowd and do the expected thing and blindly subject ourselves to the will of the populace. We should belong to a church for the sake of belonging to a church. I responded to her by posing the question *should I do that if I don't really believe in what the church has to say? Is it okay for me to stand in the pews every Sunday and mindlessly repeat a bunch of things that I don't really think are right? And are considerations like these less important than the need to conform to what all the neighbors do and so that we can participate in the social facets of a church body?*

Is the big idea behind church simply to have no one notice my car in the driveway on Sunday mornings?

My mother always taught me – as good mothers do – to be honest and truthful with myself and with others. To be authentic and *my own man.* And so, when I posed my issue to her in this fashion, she could readily begin to see the very real problem that confronted me. Certainly I would never wish for my children to meet with the silly accusatory fingers that might point their way at school or in their social circles. And these fearsome condemnations have surely come – both of my children have been told by classmates and even the parents of friends that they are destined to burn in hell. But at some point, we must hold ourselves to a higher standard and stand firm in our belief of what is real and what is not. To me, that is the truest test of faith.

Ironically, I find that we enjoy a full-blown daily discourse in our household about God and spirituality and how these ideas need to manifest themselves in our daily lives. I sense a very real God-consciousness within my family and throughout our home. Perhaps because we don't focus solely on checking off the box marked "God" after attending a regular Sunday morning motivational rally at the local megachurch, we are able to keep the fire of curiosity and discussion burning more brightly throughout the week. And maybe because we do not limit our discussions of the nature of the Divine to a carefully defined set of limited views, we are able to focus on the real issues that lie at the core of humanity's desire for relevance and meaning and faith and try to live our lives the best we can each day. The way that the God we each know would want us to.

The mystique that has come to surround the very real morality plays that make up our Oracle and our books of knowledge is a strong and imposing force – powerful enough, in fact, to blind us to the reality that these are words on pages and nothing more. We simply state that something has come from a work such as the Bible or the Torah or the Koran, and we invoke an aura that sets up a wall to defend what is said against even the most honest critical inquiry. Social dynamics plays a part, too. Stand in a group of five thousand people who all believe that we are supposed to wear green socks because a sacred and holy dictum says so, and we're fairly likely to put on green socks.

Back aboard the asteroid, Kirk and Spock managed to unlock the mystery of the Oracle and its book of knowledge and reprogram the spaceship just in time to avoid its impending catastrophe. In doing so, they left behind a more enlightened people with a new freedom to steer their own course to paradise. Interestingly, they found useful bits of information within the book of knowledge that helped to cure McCoy of a mysterious disease that would have soon claimed his life – leaving us with the unavoidable truth that all sacred works do contain great practical wisdom. In the end, the crew of the Enterprise continued on its mission to *boldly go where no man has gone before,* leaving behind a moral lesson – and yet another broken heart.

Here on Earth, others who claim to speak for God will continue to grovel for crumbs or beg for mercy or interpret the meanings of the sacred books in all sorts of strange ways. Who's to argue? That's far too exhausting and nobody wins. Instead, I will remind myself that the Oracle of the Star Trek episode was little more than a short metal can with blinking lights, banged out with hammers in some workshop on the studio back lot the night before the shoot, and continue to seek the God that works for me.

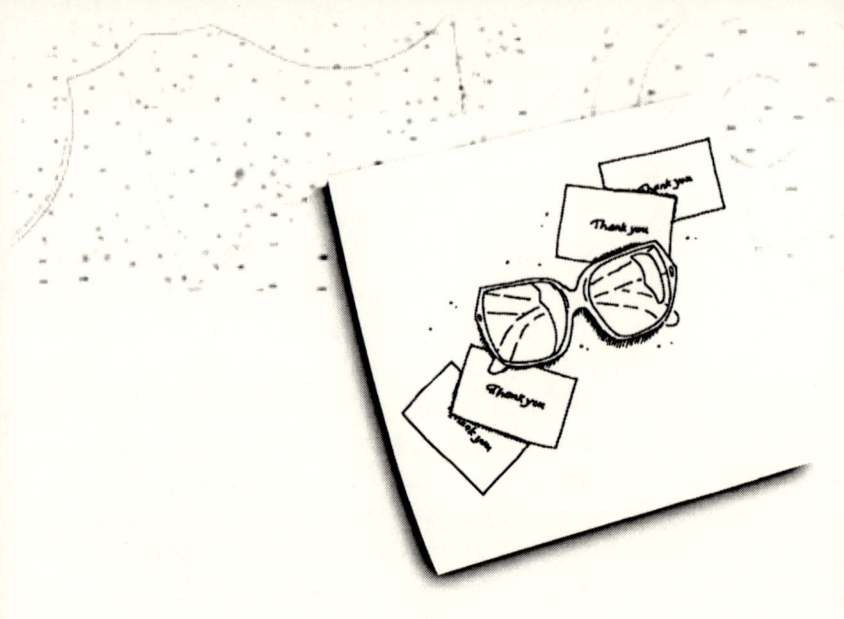

Sixteen: Children's Stories

Nurse Margaret was short and stout, with glasses that seemed far too large perched atop a small ski-slope nose and silver hair pulled tightly into a bun on the back of her head. She had a kindly demeanor and steady smile but carried herself always as if she meant business, which, of course, she always did. She was a senior nurse at a children's hospital and had been assigned to be my primary clinical contact for a series of stories I was writing for the hospital's new magazine. Once vetted through the hospital's marketing department and given the obligatory tour of the facility, I had been passed off to Nurse Margaret – who would be my handler, responsible for pointing me to doctors and research and interview sources. Working from my list, I called her to get the wheels turning on my first story, a feature about Cystic Fibrosis.

"What do you know about cystic fibrosis?" she asks. "Not much," I tell her. I only know that it is a disease that affects mostly children. I recall going to grade school with a boy who had cystic fibrosis who sometimes wheezed and had trouble breathing and often left during class to go to the nurse's office. I remember that he never stayed after school for band or sports and never played hard with the other kids. Nurse Margaret tells me that the hospital has a major program for the treatment and study of Cystic Fibrosis – CF – one of the best centers in the nation, in fact. She sends me some information, which I duly read. And then she sets up a time for me to come and visit with a few doctors and see some of the children. She tells me that I should be sure to spend some time with one patient in particular, a young man named John who had been around the program for quite a while. "He's one of the older ones," she tells me. "He'll have some pretty good insights for you."

Several days later, I arrive at the hospital to do the interviews, and I am led to a large center, a ward of its own, several floors up and toward the rear of the hospital. By now I know at least something about the broad basics of CF – the facts and the science – but I am ready to see the human side of it. The main room is large and colorful and playfully decorated – *the way it should be for kids,* I tell myself. I see the children, many of whom live at the center nearly all of the time, or at least stay for extended periods when they need the intensive breathing and massage treatments that will help them process and expel the thick mucus-like fluids that build up in their lungs. I meet with the doctor who heads the program and then talk with several of the nurses. I gather the data – numbers and statistics and other details that will add depth and breadth to the story. When I am done, one of the nurses leads me down a long hallway to meet with John.

Getting ready to round the corner into John's room, I put on my happy game face, the kind we all use when we're about to interact with children. But when I enter the room and see John sitting upright in the bed, I am taken aback. He is in his late twenties or perhaps even his early thirties, with long brown hair and a black T-shirt emblazoned with the logo of a heavy metal band. The stubble across his face leads downward to a bushy little shrub attached at the chin. His eyes are bright and smiling and he sticks out his hand to greet me. "Bet you thought I was going to be younger," he says. I get the feeling that he is quite used to surprising strangers like me.

Meeting John catches me completely off guard, tossing me for a quick loop. Yes, I had expected someone much younger – maybe a teenager at the top end. And right off the bat I think everything I have learned about CF seems null and void. I smile back and reach out to shake his hand. "Yes, I guess I was – what are you, seventeen, eighteen?" He grins and I grin, too. It strikes me that at this point in my life I am only a few years older than he is. And we obviously have the same tastes in rock bands. So we start by talking about music – a mutual passion – and then we wander into other parts of his life and eventually into the genetic disease that has defined most of it. Over the course of two hours he tells me his story – the tale of a young man defying the odds to reach an age he never expected to see. He gives me volumes of insight about CF from a patient's point of view. He has seen and lived it all.

At one point during our meeting, a young boy peers around the doorway and then slowly walks into the room. He seems sad and depressed. John furrows his brow and shows a serious face and beckons the boy over to hop up on the side of the bed. John talks to the boy reassuringly, telling him that if he feels sad then he will soon feel happy again and that he should not focus on the bad things that worry him. I sense that John is the elder statesman on the floor, the one who shows the others – the children – how to pull themselves up by their bootstraps and put forth a positive attitude. I think of Rufio, the King of the Lost Boys, from Stephen Spielberg's Peter Pan adaptation *Hook* – a boy who grows to become a man himself by caring for the other lost boys who surround him. After a minute or two of pep talk, John tousles the boy's hair and sends him on his way.

"I'm very stern with them when they need it," he says. "There is absolutely no room up here for moping around and feeling sorry for yourself. It can bring the whole place down in no time – nobody likes that." I sense that John has learned this by going through an endless string of ups and downs himself and discovering, ultimately, that positive always beats pain in the long run. Through that experience, he has given himself the mantel of chief counselor and big brother to all the children in the center. John nods toward the door after the boy leaves. "I have nothing to lose, and so I try to help them in any way I can – I know what they're going through."

He goes on to tell me that he never expected to see his fifteenth birthday, or his twentieth. When he turned twenty-five, he had become an anomaly and made a conscious decision to use the gift of his extra time for research and experimentation. Seeing each new day as a step into the unknown, he offered himself up as a research subject at CF clinics around the country. He spent months at a laboratory in Bethesda, Maryland and at the Centers for Disease Control and Prevention in Atlanta, Georgia where he underwent excruciating new experimental treatments. He eagerly volunteered to try new medicines and procedures. And he was standing at the ready for other new opportunities as they arose.

A technician comes in to tell John that it's time to get ready for his own afternoon treatment, and so we wrap up our interview. I thank him for his time, and he asks me when the story will be finished. I tell him that I don't know –

a month or two, maybe – but I will do my best to make sure that he gets a few copies of the magazine. "Don't take too long," he says, smiling. "You never know."

The next day I call Nurse Margaret to follow up. "So what did you think of John?" she asks. "An amazing guy," I tell her. "Yes," she says. "Quite a story." I make a note to myself to always pump her for more information before heading out to do future interviews. I don't yet know her well enough to tell her that calling John *an amazing guy* is perhaps the understatement of my year. I realize that of all the things I think I have offered to all of the people in my life, I have never done anything that comes close to what John is doing every day. And I am already beginning to wonder who will learn more – the readers or me – from the stories I am writing.

My next story is about neonatal surgery – the ability to perform delicate operations on babies while they are still in their mother's womb. Again Nurse Margaret loads me up with information and plugs me into doctors who I am to interview. I study with fascination how new procedures allow surgeons to repair tiny hearts and lungs and other internal organs so that babies have better survival rates and fewer problems after birth. I arrive at the unit early one afternoon to interview a doctor who is considered to be a pioneer in the field. A nurse at the counter points to him through several rooms divided by panes of glass and tells me that he may be a little late. He strikes me as young – maybe mid-thirties, tops. I had expected someone much older. From where I am standing I cannot tell exactly what he is doing, but I see that he has his arms extended up to the elbows through rubber gloves into a sealed acrylic box of some sort. I have seen devices like this in factories that use hazardous chemicals, but I speculate that the doctor is working with something altogether different.

He stands at the chamber for an hour, and I continue waiting. While I wait, I think about the other assignments

I have for the day. I am behind on deadlines and growing more so by the minute. I begin to feel mildly frustrated and wonder if I should reschedule for another time. I start to think that maybe this doctor isn't taking our appointment as seriously as I am.

When he finally comes out, he smiles, we shake hands, and he apologizes for keeping me waiting. "Want some coffee?" he asks. "Sure," I say, so we head down a hallway to the doctors' lounge. He is upbeat and exuberant as he explains the intricate details of operating on one tiny body buried deeply within another. He has tremendous enthusiasm for what he and his colleagues are able to do. I ask him what the great challenges are, what makes this so dramatically different from other forms of very small and detailed surgeries? "Imagine wet tissue paper," he says. "That's what fetal intestines are like – and we are able to repair them and suture them up when they're snarled or blocked – that's quite a challenge." He has captured my attention; this is some pretty neat stuff. But I also remember my other deadlines – projects I have promised but not yet delivered. And so I find a way to cut the interview short and tell him that perhaps we can follow up on details by phone. "Fine," he says.

On the way out, the doctor stops at the counter to look back through the panes of glass to the room where he had been working earlier. Others are there working now. "Again, I'm sorry I kept you waiting," he says. "No problem," I say. "What exactly is going on back there," I ask. "We're working on a *preemie*," he tells me – a premature baby. "We're all talking turns massaging his heart. Might not make it."

Once again I follow up with Nurse Margaret, and she wants to know what I have learned. "We talked all about microsurgery," I tell her. "I think I have everything I need to write the story – thanks and I'll let you know if there's anything else." I do not tell her about the doctor palpitating a tiny little heart to keep a tiny little human alive, or that

I felt terrible for drawing him away from that. I do not tell her that my sense of my own selfish priorities and self-importance had taken a serious hit the day before – for nothing that I do in my daily life comes close to cradling the life of a little infant in my hands.

The next month Nurse Margaret gets me set up for a story that sounds much more mechanical – a write-up on a new imaging machine that can look inside the human body by making a thousand tiny vertical pictures. This system – very commonplace now – will enable doctors to look for problems and diagnose issues with extreme detail. She tells me whom to contact, and I make arrangements with the doctor who has been behind the drive to acquire this marvelous new mass of machinery. It has been his baby, and he is proud to show it off. We meet and he guides me into a darkened room full of computer monitors. Through a large plate glass window, I look into a much bigger room and see what looks like the Apollo Lunar Landing Module. I remember grainy black and white TV images of the craft as it sat on the moon's surface, and there it stands before me – a large white pod-like structure with lots of oblique angles and anchored on four big legs. There is a large hollow tube that runs through it from side to side, with a table that leads up to the opening at one end.

The doctor tells me in great detail how the machine works. "Imagine slicing a huge bologna sausage into pieces so thin you could see through them," he says. "We are able to do that and then look at each slice on these monitors," he adds, pointing to the big screens at workstations all around. He reaches over to a keyboard and types something and up pop some sample images. He taps a key and moves through them quickly so that the images change in sequence like the early movies I remember from an antique kinescope in a museum somewhere. Blobs within the images change shape and size and tint as they go by.

As we are talking, the doctor's cell phone rings and he takes the call. His mood quickly changes as he shifts gears from magazine article-mode back to imaging specialist. He talks in hushed tones for thirty seconds and then snaps the phone shut. "Looks like we'll get to see it in action," he tells me. That's a good thing, I think – a demonstration will allow me to add a human element to the story and learn more about how the machine actually works, too. In my mind, a demo says a thousand words.

Ten minutes later, the darkened control room is brightly lit and full of people – nurses, technicians and other doctors begin to filter in. I take a quiet place in the corner where I can be invisible and watch and take notes. Out in the room with the big machine, the doors swing open and a young girl is wheeled in on a gurney. She looks to be maybe eight or nine, with long blonde hair and a face full of freckles. Her bright blue eyes are wide open, and she looks terrified as they lift her from the gurney to the table that will shuttle her through the lunar module one tiny step at a time. As I watch, the doctor comes over to tell me that just that morning the girl had complained of difficulty breathing over breakfast. Unable to find an obvious reason – no chest cold or asthma – her pediatrician had sent her straight to the hospital hoping that this marvelous new gizmo might provide answers.

Moments later the machine begins its work, firing up with a series of noises that sound like sledge hammers banging on metal drums. The door opens to the now-crowded room I share with the doctors, and a man and woman enter, looking worried – obviously the girl's parents. From where I am in the corner, I can peer under an arm and over a shoulder to see the blotchy black and white images that appear on the screens. The doctors fold their arms and stare. Occasionally, one reaches out to point at something on a monitor and mumbles. Heads nod. After a few more minutes, my contact comes over to me and tells me that we will need to finish our talk at another time. I glance over at the monitors where I plainly see a big black blob running from frame to frame, growing larger in each image. A tumor the size of a football fills her chest cavity, he tells me. As I leave the room, I glance quickly at the father and mother, who are not looking at the monitors but are instead holding tightly to each other. The mother is fighting back tears.

The next day when I talk to Nurse Margaret, I tell her about the little girl with the blues eyes and blond hair and the parents and the big black blob on the screens. "That's part of what we see everyday – you get used to it," she says. But then she perks up and adds, "Isn't it great that we have that machine?" Yes, it's wonderful, I tell her. But I am truly not thinking of the machine. I am still thinking about the parents and the little blonde-haired girl with a face full of freckles. I have a daughter roughly the same age.

Over time we work on maybe a dozen stories – Nurse Margaret and I – each taking me farther and farther into a world of sensitivities I had not known. Each story leaves its mark on me and makes me wonder about suffering and children and why the two subjects always seem to collide in the same places at the same times.

Our work culminates with a big feature on Nurse Margaret's personal area of specialization – pediatric intensive care. I meet with *her* this time, *she* is my subject, and I am out to learn all there is to know about a state-of-the-art new pediatric ICU, one of the best of its type in the country. This is her domain, her primary beat, her real day-to-day job. As a nursing supervisor, she calls many of the shots here. The new unit is a large circular space with a giant nursing and administrative station at the center and a dozen or more patient rooms making up the outer ring. Each room has a full wall of glass facing the middle so that the staff can keep an eyeball on patients at all times. Each room is crammed with expensive-looking equipment – it hangs from the ceilings and walls and stands on wheeled pedestals. The rooms are alive with blips and bleeps, and there seem to be little red or green lights blinking everywhere.

As we walk and talk around the big circle – she pointing out items of interest and me jotting down notes – I take a casual look into one of the rooms. I have my game face on, so I am focused on the facts, glued to the story. But the occupant of this room catches my eye. He is a young boy, perhaps ten or eleven. He lies in the bed with his head slightly elevated and with tubes coming out of his nose and mouth. His arms are at his side and also tied up in tubing and tape. But above all of this, I can see that his hair is curly and brown and his eyes are bright and blue. He is looking straight at me, watching me. I do not know why I connect with this one boy when I have seen so many others over the course of my stories, but I do. He is looking directly at me, and I can very clearly hear the question that he is asking me through his eyes – *why am I here in this bed and not outside in the sunshine and throwing a baseball or chasing frogs or hitting things with sticks like boys do?*

I have developed a good working relationship with Nurse Margaret. We like each other and there is a sense of trust between us. But up until now, our relationship has been all business. I have never had the courage to tell her how deeply I have been affected by each of the stories we have worked on. I have never in our discussions gone beneath the level of facts and information and insights. I have never taken our conversation to the human level – to talk about the life and death and hurt and healing that she and the others around her must see every day.

I notice an assortment of Thank You cards laid out on the counter at the nurses' station next to a small vase of flowers. She notices me looking at them and leaps ahead of my question, telling me that the flowers and cards have come from the family of a child who died in the unit several days earlier. "I'm sorry – how often does that happen here?" I ask.

"Often enough," she says. "The children who come here are the ones fighting the toughest battles."

I think about the boy in the bed with the tubes and the tape, and I decide to ask Nurse Margaret what I have wanted to know for months. I look around the unit and see half a dozen nurses moving about, going in and out of rooms, doing all the many things that nurses do. They are stoic and professional and mostly expressionless. I think that Nurse Margaret is waiting for my question. "How do you do it?" I ask. "How do you cope with losing so many…"

Nurse Margaret cuts me off instantly, leaning forward and staring at me through the too-large glasses that sit atop her ski-slope nose. She reaches out and touches my arm, then shakes her head slowly side to side. "We never focus on the loss," She says. "We spend our time and our energy doing what we can to help – we focus on making these kids comfortable, easing their pain and doing everything we can to serve them. We learn early on that you can't save them all – the gift we can give is in relieving the suffering." This is a perspective that I have never considered.

"So you must simply have to work to suppress the feelings," I say, and again she cuts me off. "How is that possible? The pain and suffering we feel is what drives the care and compassion we work to give," she says. I look at Nurse Margaret and again at the nurses moving about and doing their jobs on the ward. I see them differently. I wonder if perhaps they have been called to do this work – God knows there are other jobs that come with more money and far less heartache. I think that it is no accident that nurses are often referred to as *angels of mercy.*

Over the course of the nearly fifteen years since I worked so closely with Nurse Margaret, I have come to believe that she was quite right in her assessment of pain and suffering in our world. She was wise, as most old nurses are. For there is no such thing as a world without anguish.

Religions tell us that Heaven is a place without suffering – that our broken bodies and spirits will be made whole and we will know eternal bliss. Even my favorite Buddhist monk tells me that the ultimate quest for each of us is the search for a Pure Land where there is no pain, no suffering. But I do not think that is possible, or right, or even desirable. I believe we are supposed to have pain and suffering – for it is in our personal places of hurt and want that we are most exposed to the goodness of the world and the people around us. Suffering gives us an opportunity to practice compassion. Pain gives us the chance to care and heal.

    I have learned that with every positive in life, there must always be a negative. Any air-conditioning repairman will tell you that cold is simply the absence of heat – the compressors and condensers that cool our homes do so by removing heat from the air. A glass is never either half full or half empty as many people say – it is completely full all the time. Knowing that, I do not think that I would want to live in a world without suffering, for without it I could never know joy and happiness. Perhaps that is why Mother Teresa chose to live out her personal spiritual ministry atop the garbage heaps of Calcutta – for there is where she felt most exposed to the vast and awesome potential of God's goodness.

    I have also learned that we are supposed to feel with great sensitivity. Better still, I want to. I have always felt that I was somehow born with my nerve endings on the outside, exposed to everything, overly susceptible to every emotion. I cry at movies – and I am glad that I do, for it means that I can feel freely. I know that when I live my life with my receptors set wide open, every frequency tuned to the raw emotion and feeling of the world about me, with the amplifier knobs set to *eleven,* then I am living life to its fullest – closest to the God that I know. Many of us labor our entire lives to suppress our feelings. But, in doing so, we perhaps miss out on one of life's biggest blessings, one of God's greatest gifts. Like wise old nurses who see pain and suffering as opportunities to share love and compassion, we are supposed to stand upright and steadfast in the breath of the dragon in order to be closest to a God who truly works through us.

I believe that many among us have been blessed with what I tell my daughter is the *artist's heart*. It is a gift no doubt – for it gives us a broadband connection to the immense spiritual power of the universe. But it can also be a curse – for some are never able to harness it properly or keep it reasonably constrained. I have stood near the spot outside of Arles in the Provence region of southern France where Vincent van Gogh painted his masterwork *Starry Night*. Looking up at the brilliant dots of light, hung in their full majesty above the sunflowers and lavender fields of that beautiful country, I can readily understand van Gogh's insanity. Historians may blame it on the lead and toxic chemicals in his hand-mixed paints, but I know differently. His artist's heart was simply overloaded. His world may have been simply too beautiful for his senses to bear.

The vast majority of the work I do in my business is dry and sterile and practical and – quite frankly – often boring. Yes, I write about important things – new electronic gizmos that make life somehow better, or food products that are healthier for us, and building materials that make stronger, longer-lasting structures, and banking services that help spenders spend and savers save. But of all the things I have worked on over a period of twenty-five years, nothing has affected me like the series of stories I wrote with Nurse Margaret. She taught me about the fullness and wholeness of life. She showed me that without suffering there can be no healing.

And, without knowing it, she helped to heal a part of me, too.

Seventeen: Getting There From Here

As a college student, I spent many summer months working offshore in the Gulf of Mexico aboard deep-sea tugboats like the *Mister Randy*. I was the lowest form of life in the Merchant Marine – a deckhand – and the oil fields off the coasts of Louisiana and Texas were a great place to pick up great spending money for school and stay out of trouble – mostly – at the same time. Aboard these workboats – sturdy little vessels perhaps some ninety to one hundred feet in length – we stayed far out at sea for many weeks at a time. It was often round-the-clock work and, as an all-purpose *swabbie*, I worked two six-hour watches per day.

My chosen watches were noon until six in the evening, and midnight to six in the morning. This latter shift was by far my favorite. As often as not, we spent the quiet hours of the early "dog watch" tied up to a sea buoy. The boat was usually quieter than normal – the captain, cook and engineers were all asleep, and unless there was serious work to be done, the mate would nod off in the chair in the wheelhouse and leave us deckhands to handle the ship's housekeeping duties. Once this was done – usually in just a couple of hours – I would climb to the highest parts of the vessel and find a quiet place to sit and watch the stars. Anybody who has ever witnessed the beauty of a clear night sky out in the middle of the ocean appreciates the difficulty I find in coming up with words that adequately describe the beauty and magnificence of it all. I think poets and mariners throughout history have come up short in even the most lavish descriptions.

I will always remember in particular one midsummer night when we received a radio call to pick up a massive barge of large-diameter pipe tethered to a buoy in the middle of nowhere and tow it many miles away to a waiting construction ship. I quickly volunteered to hop across to the pipe barge and rig up the heavy steel bridle and towline. Once this was done, the cook appeared at the railing of the tugboat and tossed across a duffel bag containing a few sandwiches, a thermos of coffee and some emergency gear. As the ship motored off into the distance, paying out perhaps a mile of two-inch cable, I climbed to the top of the huge pyramid of stacked pipe. Reaching the crown, I laid back, spread out my feast, and enjoyed what will always rank among the finest few hours of my entire life.

I was surrounded by beauty – the sight of countless stars spanning the sky from horizon to horizon, the sounds of water rushing past as the heavy barge plodded on through the vast empty ocean, the far distant rumbling of the throaty diesel engines aboard the tug, the quick glimpses of flying fish that leapt from the sea and skimmed for hundreds of feet just across the wave-tops under the moonlight, the feel of the warm gulf breeze, and the wonderful smell of the cook's unimaginably strong coffee. It all combined to create one of the most incredibly peaceful and overwhelming experiences my senses have ever encountered. I can only pray that Heaven – or the next life, whatever it may be – will be something similar.

It's not hard to have an experience like that – a brief moment in time that can and will be relived over and over again in my memory until the day I die – and truly believe that we are in the hands of a loving and wonderful Creator. I no longer care who or what God is. I do not have to create a definition or read a book or subscribe to a set of tenets in order to feel the immensity of it all in my heart. I do not have to believe the way somebody else believes, or try to make them believe as I do. It is enough simply for me to believe. It is enough for me to have a faith that is my very own – one that makes perfect sense to me.

I had the opportunity several years ago to help two friends – a husband and wife – sail their yacht up from Corpus Christi to Galveston Bay, a trip that would take about a day, maybe a few hours more. They had a beautiful boat – a tricked-out forty-one-footer that I had sailed on before in various coastal bays – so when the chance came to join them for some true blue water sailing, I jumped. The trip would require us to head far out to sea and then weave our way northeast along a designated "highway" in the sea – a route marked on charts only – that winds it's way through the hundreds of oil and gas platforms and well-heads that dot the Gulf of Mexico like sausage trees on the Serengeti Plain of central Africa. We left at mid-day, and as soon as the flat Texas shoreline disappeared behind our stern, we set up four-hour watches at the helm. This would leave one of us in charge of monitoring the radar, adjusting the autopilot and listening to the radio while the other two were free to move about or go below to rest or eat. I quickly volunteered for the midnight watch, eager to relive the mid-ocean starry sky memories from my summers aboard tugboats nearly three decades earlier.

When midnight came, I perched myself up on the high side of the cockpit at the transom, so that I could tilt my head back and gaze out from under the canvas top to see the stars glowing wildly from the heavens above. Hours earlier, the sky had been overcast and I had worried that I might miss my chance to see my sparkling friends. But now the clouds had melted away, leaving a deep blue dome overhead that sprawled from horizon to horizon dotted with a million glittering diamonds.

Off in the distance where the water met the sky in every direction I could see blinking lights and hear muffled horns and bells of various pitches and patterns – markers for all the towering platforms that rose from the sea. I used these to double-check our position, periodically checking the radar to see our course safely plotted through the bright blips on the screen that matched up to what I could hear with my ears and see with my eyes. The northerly breeze was light but steady, and we moved along at a comfortable six or seven knots, leaning ever so slightly over to starboard. The motion of the waves was gentle and peaceful and relaxing. I kept my eye on the radar and on our plot and occasionally checked the set of the sails to be sure we were getting the most out of the moderate winds.

But it was the stars that I truly wanted to see – because they cannot be studied like this anywhere close to where I live three hundred miles inland on the outskirts of a large and brightly lit city. It was late in the summer, the time of year when the most recognizable constellations appear in the Western Hemisphere, so there was much to see in the night skies above. There was also a new moon – barely a sliver low over the eastern horizon. So the challenge that confronted me wasn't a lack of stars, but an overabundance of stellar bodies in the sky. There were far too many stars, and they were all far too bright, for me to easily make out the celestial objects that I can normally spot in an instant out in the city suburbs.

Using our compass, I found the North Star – Polaris – and used it as my starting point. Moving south, I passed through Cassiopeia, the "Queen's Chair," which looks like a giant letter M lying sideways, and picked out the three bright stars that make up the Summer Triangle – Deneb, Vega and Altair. From there I knew where to pick out the giant flying swan that the ancients dubbed Cygnus.

Moving across the sky to the southeast, I eyed one of the most recognizable constellations in the sky – Orion, the Hunter. Orion's two brightest corners – a shoulder and a knee – are the giant red star Betelgeuse – "Beetlejuice" – and blue-hot Rigel. I spotted the three consecutive stars that make up Orion's belt, with its sword dangling southward. I knew that the middle star of the belt – Alnilam – always sits directly above the equator. And I knew that the middle star of the sword isn't a star at all but rather the Orion Nebula, which is a fantastic, massive red cloud of dust and gas that serves as a galactic nursery – a mother to thousands of infant stars over the course of many millions of years.

Moving south and east on a straight line through the belt, I easily spotted Sirius – the Dog Star – the brightest star in the sky. And from there I made a wide swinging arc back to the north through Procyon – the Little Dog Star – and then through Castor and Pollux – the famous twins of Gemini – and finally to Capella, whom the ancients called the mother sheep because she keeps constant watch over three tiny lambs.

Drawing a line with my eyes from Polaris back down to Alnilam, I moved at right angles in both directions through a broad swath of sky that generally follows the plane of our solar system and quickly picked out several large, bright objects that did not twinkle as stars do. These are planets – "rovers" to the ancients – Jupiter, surrounded by its many moons, and Saturn, which appeared oblong because of its almost-visible rings. I knew that Venus – alternately called the Morning Star or the Evening Star because its orbit lies between Earth and the Sun and will always appear either at dawn or dusk – would begin its rise in a few hours in the east with the brightness of a halogen headlight.

And, finally, moving northwest through Orion's belt, I spotted the flaming red eye of Taurus, the Bull – Aldebaran – and then the tiny dense cluster of stars that make up Pleiades. This group is often mistaken for the Little Dipper, but is, in fact, the *seven sisters* who can be seen in the logo on the back of every Subaru automobile.

Leaning back in the fresh night air and taking in as much of this overhead majesty as possible – my own private planetarium – I began to ponder the idea of Heaven. I have often wondered why we point and stare upward to the skies above when we speak of Heaven or invoke the blessings of God or think of the dearly departed. I've flown as high as most humans ever go in an airplane, read dozens of books about space flight and rocket launches, and followed with great interest the magic of the Hubble Space Telescope, but I have yet to see one single harp or set of pearly gates floating on the clouds above.

But have I seen Heaven, *really?* Actually, I think so. Anyone who has looked to the east early on a clear autumn morning – particularly out on the ocean – and has seen how the thin stripe of red begins to glow and change to broader stripes of purple, orange, pink, gold and finally bold and bright yellows has caught a glimpse of the Pure Land we might think of as Heaven. We imagine that God's realm – the holding company for everything that is truly magical and mysterious and marvelous about our world – must surely reside in a place as amazing as the early morning sky. So why not point upward when we speak of the unexplained? Who has a better answer? I suppose that if I have to have a place where I might find the souls of my brother and mother, it should be as beautiful and powerful and magnificent as that.

Since I learned to sail as a youth, I've spent lots of time – with a few years off here and there – studying the traditions and sciences that surround sailing. Celestial navigation has always intrigued me – so much so that ten years ago I signed up for a course to get my celestial navigation certification. As a writer and pretty much right-brained person, I had always struggled through as little math as possible and had avoided altogether brain-jarring courses like spherical trigonometry. But when it came to really wanting to understand how celestial navigation worked – and to actually be able to do it myself – I found that learning all those complicated equations came pretty easily. A willing and eager pupil can pick up almost anything.

But along with this fascination with plotting lines of position and computing right-hour angles came a true desire to learn the cosmos. I had seen all those stars running from horizon to horizon on warm, moonless nights out on the ocean years before and had always wanted to learn the various constellations. Orion, Sagittarius, Scorpius, Pegasus, the big and little dippers – they all fascinated me. And it seemed – still does – incredible and amazing to me that ancient seafarers could find their way across vast oceans simply by understanding the relative positions and motions of these heavenly bodies. So in typical obsessive-compulsive fashion, I dove in headfirst, amassing a sizeable library of books on stars, planets, nebulas, galaxies, and everything related. I developed a fairly solid idea of how the universe works, with orbits and rotations and phases. All of which has an undeniable spiritual bent.

I read somewhere that – in what might seem an ultimate paradox to some – many of our world's most widely acclaimed physicists, astronomers, mathematicians and scientists are deeply spiritual people. It might seem contradictory to some that these men and women of science would subscribe to any line of thought other than pure ration and reason. But I think they know there is a profound depth and beauty behind all the natural things that surround us – particularly the heavens above. Who could not try to comprehend the scope and complexity of the universe without taking a short breath in shear amazement? There's an unimaginable brilliance behind it all.

Our galaxy, the Milky Way, contains a hundred billion stars. And it's just one of millions of billions of galaxies. The size of the universe is measured in hundreds of thousands of light years – and I remember from science class that the speed of light is just over 186,000 miles per second. Consider that the light that reaches our planet from the Sun left that fiery mass just eight minutes ago; the light that reaches from top to bottom in our own very small galaxy takes sixteen thousand years – one hundred thousand light years to go from end to end. In cosmic time, the entire history of our world is but a blip. Our simple, small and humble spin on the planet Earth is a mere afterthought. To me, the immensity of it all is simply mind-boggling. It places the search for the whole idea of God into a completely different and larger realm for me.

Before the age of sophisticated electronic computers and global-positioning systems, mariners at sea lived in one of two worlds of navigation. If they were inland or along a coastline – or anywhere they could see fixed points of reference like a lighthouse, a headland, or even a marked buoy out of sight of land – they could use simple tools like a compass and protractor to triangulate exactly where they were in relation to those objects. This *coastal navigation* is basically the science of using what is known about objects that don't move – or at least it is *hoped* they don't move – to determine the position of a moving vessel relative to land. If, on the other hand, they were far out to sea and away from any fixed points of reference, navigators were forced to rely on anything they could find. This typically meant celestial bodies – the sun, the moon, the planets or the many stars that become visible just as the sun rises or sets. The problem with using celestial navigation is that, like the vessel that the navigator is hoping to guide, the objects in the sky are moving, too. They are never fixed.

Learning to follow only the God that we already know is much like navigating along the shore – using fixed points of reference that have been plotted out for us long ago by the explorers who came before. They took the time to build the lighthouses and anchor the buoys and survey the depths so that we could comfortably and easily find our way to a safe harbor. Others have done the hard work for us – they have defined everything – so that if we follow the directions they have left for us then we can fairly confidently move from port to port. There is little work and even less risk involved. The problem with this is that we are forever confined to the shoreline. We are limited to what we can see and what is already familiar to us. We deny ourselves the opportunity to explore the different and exotic new worlds that may lie far away beyond the horizon. We are limited to the world we know and unable to range off on our own to discover the new worlds waiting across the seas.

Heading off on our own voyage of spiritual discovery is much like leaving the safety and comfort of a known shore. We will have to rely on the continual variation of objects that we may recognize, but that are also changing and moving. Shorelines and harbor landmarks will not move; they are safe and widely recognized. But celestial bodies are never the same – their positions in relation to us on the surface of the earth, as well as to each other, are in constant flux. In fact, they will all be in the very same places exactly once – *right now, this very second* – and then they will forever be different. Learning the science – arguably it's more of an art – of navigating by the signposts in the heavens above requires much more courage than simple coastal navigation.

We need to be comfortable with the idea of moving beyond what we can see and what we have known. We need to be fearless, willing to believe that guiding lights will enable us to find our way in places where none have ventured before. And we also need to have faith that we will not fall off the ends of the earth in our search to find potentially wondrous new destinations.

One of the little-known pearls of genius that makes Christopher Columbus such a hero to navigators was his unwavering belief that a new continent lay stretched out beyond the western horizon. Against all conventional wisdom, he *knew* that land lay far out beyond the setting sun. But he bolstered his faith with a few keen observations. Living as he did at the latitudes of the Mediterranean, he saw for himself how the trade winds and currents flowed constantly westward. *Where did they go*, he wondered? He had sailed far enough north in his wanderings to learn that the Gulf Stream delivered that same wind and current back to Europe around the latitude of the British Isles – in fact, Ireland is called the Emerald Isle because of the lush green vegetation that grows along its western shore, a product of warm waters and fresh, mild breezes. While others believed that the southerly trades would take him out to the edge of the earth and then over the side and into the abyss, he had faith enough to believe that courage, curiosity and the willingness to do what others said couldn't be done would bring its own rewards. He trusted his own personal intuition, but he also had faith enough to believe that more could be learned about our world. And if more could be learned about the earth, then perhaps more could be understood about God. He prayed. He sailed. And he discovered.

Like Columbus, with his well-founded speculation that winds and water that flowed to the west must eventually return to the east – flowing back from some far-off new land – I have learned to believe in things that seem to go against what I can detect with my senses or that others who have gone before might tell me. I have learned that in order to explore a spiritual world and pinpoint an understanding of a working God that falls outside the boundaries of markers that have been staked out on the shoreline by skippers long centuries ago, I can trust in things that I may not sense, things that I must determine on my own and to my own exact satisfaction. I will follow my own stars. And, like Columbus, I have learned that on top of all the knowledge I might gain in my travels and training, I also must have faith.

I find lots of peace – and acceptance – in the idea that I am powerless in God's massive, almost never-ending world. The notion that I am but a mere handful of atoms in a cosmos so large that the light-wave radiation from the original Big Bang is only now reaching the edge of the universe – traveling at that mind-numbing 186,000 miles per second – enthralls and amazes me. I'm perfectly okay with the thought that I have an infinitely limited understanding of God's Big Plan – and can never really hope to have much more than that. At least not on this Earthly plane.

Back aboard the yacht, cruising steadily northeast under the canopy of the night sky's majesty, I breathed in the warm night air and marveled at the beauty and mystery of the private lightshow that entertained me from above. I was surprised at how challenging it had been for me to draw out a handful of celestial bodies that I know so well from the background of tens of thousands of stars that I normally do not see. It had taken effort.

But I was comforted by the knowledge that they are there – and will always be there to guide me – like God – if I am only willing to look.

Afterword: Signposts and Lessons

I love windshield time. Driving along an open stretch of highway on a sunny afternoon with the windows down and radio and cell phone turned off, I allow my mind to wander, racing like the wind to work through the countless thoughts that make up the background noise of my mental being. Religion and faith have become topics that I hear about – in a dozen various ways – each and every day. In recent years, the volume has risen slowly, almost imperceptibly, to a level that cannot be easily ignored. And the many inputs I receive are as varied as the wide world of religion itself – sometimes they are topics of global importance, and just as often they are tiny little tidbits of trivial information that pertain to hardly anything at all. But collectively, they make up one of the largest – if not *the* largest – gatherings of background clutter in my mind.

On one occasion, for some unknown reason, all those many separate elements of religious thought that hitchhike along in the folds of my gray matter took flight at once – like electrons swirling around an atomic nucleus – until they collided to achieve a critical mass that became impossible to ignore. The loud bang that followed shaped itself into a subject that I simply felt compelled to explore. I knew that writing this book would be the next step on my own personal spiritual adventure.

All of the many guides who had held up the spiritual signposts along my journey suddenly came together in the same place at the same moment in time – Father Martin, Nurse Margaret, the Billy Grahams and the Popes of the world, my children and their Not Me cohort, the tugboat captain, the big-haired TV preachers, my neighbors, the cab driver, the old man on the porch, Pepper-the-dog and Boston-the-cat, the boy on the bicycle, the poor woman from the church shooting, the little blonde girl with freckles, and countless others.

As the mileage markers passed by one-by-one and the sun began to settle in the west, I thought of John and his selfless giving, and Robert who taught me a new way of thinking about God over coffee, and the common everyday people who pass on quietly in the night to gain an instant understanding of the divine. I thought of the butterfly farm, the friend who had accepted my amends, and of the fish in Jerry's pet store. Memories of my days offshore and the majesty of cruising under starry night skies filled the sails of my mind. I thought of the many experiences and people who have left their marks on me – changing me, causing me to think and wonder and explore. I recalled the well-meaning lady's innocent card of condolence that had first caused me to revolt against the God I knew. And I thought of the quote I clipped from the newspaper and pinned to my office wall following the Sago Mine disaster in 2006 – a message from a little girl that reads: *"Dear God, my daddy was very special to me. I know everything happens for a reason. You just needed my daddy to fill up an empty space in your beautiful garden."*

As I rolled on through gentle hills and valleys and the brightness of a glorious day shifted to the pinks and oranges of a magnificent sunset, I reflected on the many events of my life that had suddenly happened for a reason – perhaps by order of some higher being's big plan – to bring me to the place where I needed to collect up and sort through my feelings, thoughts and ideas about faith, about religion – about God and *how the big idea of God should really work.* And, of course, all of these people, places and events were laid atop the continual daily memories I have of my brother and mother who have – perhaps divinely – guided me thus far on my journey and been my inspiration. As this wealth of gifts began to percolate through my ecstatically undisciplined mind, the lessons – which had gone unrecognized before – began to take form.

We each are unique creations of God, blessed with a direct link and empowered to develop our own understanding of who or what God is and – equally important – how God works in our lives. It is our voices from the middle ground that must now be heard in order to bring some semblance of sanity and reason to religion, which is a vital and necessary part of our human existence. We are supposed to see and feel and experience suffering because it gives us a way to measure the goodness of our world and its inhabitants. God's creation is beautiful and perfect in its chaos – and we are perfect, too – and the people who choose to speak for God and say otherwise are likewise perfect in their own humanity. And faith is a quest – an endless searching journey – that is driven by questions that we are all entitled to ask and shaped by the many gifts and lessons we gather along the way.

Breinigsville, PA USA
17 November 2009
227714BV00001B/4/P